Happily Un-Married

Living Together and Loving It

John Curtis, Ph.D.

Robert D. Reed Publishers • Bandon, OR

Robert D. Reed Publishers
P.O. Box 1992
Bandon, OR 97411
Phone: 541-347-9882; Fax: 541-347-9883
E-mail: 4bobreed@msn.com
Website: www.rdrpublishers.com

Editor: Cleone Lyvonne

Book Designer: John Curtis

Cover Designer: Cleone Lyvonne

Photo Credits for Cover, all from Dreamstime.com: *African Couple in Bed*, © Dnadigital; *Beautiful Couple in Love*, © Andresr; *Beautiful Couple*, © Digitalskillet; *Beautiful Couple in Love*, © Yuri_Arcurs; *Breakfast in Bed*, © Fotosmurf02; *Couple Watching TV*, © Iofoto; *Elderly Couple Smiling*, © Kurhan; *Happy Couple* © Lifestock Productions; *Happy Feet* © Redbaron; *In Bed*, © Diego.cervo; *In Bed*, © Diego.cervo; *Interracial Couple*, © Lucian Coman; *Senior Couple in the Kitchen*, © Mathieuviennet; *Sweet Couple in Love*, © Barsik; *Sweet Dreams*, © Yuri_Arcurs; *Young Couple in Bedroom*, © Vgstudio; *Young Couple in Love*, © Yuri_arcurs

ISBN: 978-1-934759-09-7

ISBN 10: 1-934759-09-0

Library of Congress Control Number: 2008925455

Manufactured, Typeset, and Printed in the United States of America

Table of Contents

Introduction

Are you thinking about cohabitating? Are you in such an arrangement right now? If you are feeling anxious or excited about the relationship and would like to learn some powerful strategies on how to ensure its fitness and stability, this book is for you. This book is a big departure from the typical relationship book; and if you are full of questions about what to do before cohabitating OR if you are already living together, you've come to the right place.

This book is non-judgmental; it does not attempt to build a case for or against cohabitating, whether it's an end in itself or as a stage before marriage, the decision is yours—as are the results. But it is important to understand the facts about cohabitating and how these facts may impact you. In addition, it is important to understand that...

In part, this book is designed to help you avoid the hurt, frustration, and anger that can come from bad judgment when it comes to cohabitating. This book is proactive and could be considered "fitness training" for your relationship to develop it into or keep it in the best possible condition... it is about the changing state of our unions.

WHAT IS YOUR TYPE OF COHABITATION RELATIONSHIP?
There are 20 Types of Unmarried Couples in 4 categories. Which are you?

I - Couples seeking a first-time marriage

1. *Young & in love*
2. *Conventional & ready*
3. *Pregnant & pressured*
4. *Older & independent*
5. *Him, her, & them*
6. *First love, then kids, then marriage*

II - Couples considering remarriage

7. *For one or both due to divorce (no kids)*
8. *For one or both due to divorce (with kids)*
9. *For one or both due to death (no kids)*
10. *For one or both due to death (with kids)*
11. *Reversing their own previous dissolution*

III - Low-risk cohabiting couples

12. *Pre-wedding convenience seekers*
13. *Ring-less biological parents*
14. *Trial marriage practitioners*
15. *Unmarried benefactors*

IV - High-risk cohabiting couples

16. *Relationship game players*
17. *Relationship evolutionists*
18. *Marriage-phobic resisters*
19. *Habitual cohabiters*
20. *Anti-marriage advocates*

Source Jason Krafsky

Each of these relationships is a result of many factors, and they all have unique challenges and opportunities. Regardless of which type best describes your relationship, this book provides highly relevant information and offers concrete strategies to strengthen and sustain any type of cohabitating relationship.

Cohabitation Nation

The Facts and Realities
of Living Together in America!

"It ain't so much what you don't know about cohabitation that can hurt you, it's what you do know that just ain't so —author unknown

THE FACTS!

- The U.S. Census Bureau estimates that there are currently 9.7 million Americans, or 8% of U.S. coupled households, living with an unmarried different-sex partner, 1.2 million Americans living with a same-sex partner; 11% of unmarried partners are same-sex couples,

- 41% of American women ages 15-44 have cohabited (lived with an unmarried different-sex partner) at some point. This includes 9% of women ages 15-19, 38% of women ages 20-24, 49% of women ages 25-29, 51% of women ages 30-34, 50% of women ages 35-39, and 43% of women ages 40-44,

- The number of unmarried couples living together increased 72% between 1990 and 2000,

- The number of unmarried couples living together has increased tenfold between 1960 and 2000.

Reasons for Cohabitating

- Living with someone before marriage is a way to avoid divorce and to test compatibility or establish financial security before marrying.
- Many see little difference between the commitment to live together and the commitment to marriage, and it is easier to establish and dissolve.
- Cohabiting couples do not have to seek legal or religious permission to form or dissolve their union.
- Some cohabiting couples do so to escape from family turmoil.
- Nearly half of all cohabitating couples plan to marry.
- Many cohabitate to share living expenses, to avoid loneliness, or in response to social pressure to find a mate.
- Cohabitating can be seen as a reflection of society's "do your own thing" attitude of low-commitment and high-autonomy reflected in pop culture, music, and the entertainment industry.
- Cohabitation is more common among those who are less religious.
- People who cohabit are much more likely to come from a home where their parents divorced.
- Couples from divorced families are much more likely to cohabit in an attempt to avoid the mistakes of their parents, and they often start living together at younger ages than they would typically marry.
- In many cases, living together is an understandable attempt to avoid the painful experiences of being raised in a broken home.
- Many cohabitating couples see themselves as far more independent than previous generations; and they no longer count on a committed partner for financial, physical, or emotional needs or general daily chores such as cooking and cleaning.

- Cohabitating young people feel they have greater choice, more time to choose a partner, and less of a need to make a full commitment.

Consequences of Cohabitating

- Those involved in serial cohabitation find it is easier to continually dissolve relationships, including marriages. However, those who never cohabitate but marry and divorce find it easier to file for another divorce. The failure rate of second or even third marriages bears this out.
- Most cohabitating couples who break up will end up in another cohabitating relationship.
- Women lose more than men because men tend to want younger women as their next cohabitating partner.
- If children are involved, they usually stay with the mother, which reduces her chances of finding another suitable partner.
- In addition, children continue to suffer since they are not clear about the relationship between parents and how they fit into their life.
- Religion is less likely to be an important part of the life of a cohabitating couple since, in most cases, religion does not approve of cohabitating partnerships.
- At the same time, while many cohabitating partners recognize that their living together is wrong by religious standards, they could not envision an alternative way of living.
- Cohabiting couples report being less happy and less sexually satisfied due, in part, to less monogamy among cohabitating couples.

- Cohabiting couples report feeling less connected to a community and need to make an effort to reach out to socialize with others since cohabitating couples are not as readily accepted in society, at least not yet.

- Depression among cohabiting couples is triple the rate of married couples while physical aggression happens twice as often as it does among married partners, and cohabitating women are more likely than married women to suffer physical and sexual abuse.

- 75% of children born to cohabiting parents will see their parents split up before they reach age 16 while this happens to only 1/3 of children born to married parents.

- The rise in and acceptance of cohabitation means that legal marriage is becoming one of just several alternative lifestyle choices.

- As cohabitation becomes stronger, the institution of marriage is likely to be weakened, but the gap between the two is closing as cohabiting couples increasingly gain the same legal benefits and responsibilities as married couples.

- Some claim that extending the benefits of being married condones a fragile family structure where women and children are at greater risk. On the other hand, "mainstreaming" cohabitation may also mean that society's expectations of live-in relationships will rise, pressuring cohabiting couples to be more mindful and purposeful when forming and maintaining cohabitating family units.

- Many women tend to see living together as the next step before marriage while many men see it as a sexual opportunity without the commitment.

- Current evidence does not show that living together before marriage increases the likelihood of happy and long-lasting marriages.

Trends in Cohabitation

- In much of the U.S. and Western Europe, over 50% of all marrying couples live together first.
- Cohabitation is replacing marriage as the first living-together experience for young men and women.
- There will likely be a growing surge in cohabitation since 75% of high school students believe living together is a worthwhile and harmless alternative, and over 60% of high school girls and nearly 70% of high school boys hold a favorable opinion of cohabitation.
- There has been little, if any, public opposition to cohabitation, and it is now more widely accepted than divorce or having a child out of wedlock.
- Nearly 50% of all children will spend some time in a cohabiting family before age 16.
- Cohabitating couples are seen as financially unstable, yet many of today's cohabitating couples combine their earning power and purchase a residence together.
- While many cohabitating couples are said to be unsound for raising a family, many have children together and stay together for the sake of the children.
- Many cohabitating couples lower their expectations and expect to invest less and receive less from the relationship by taking a "wait and see" attitude.

- Many cohabitating couples are actually involved in serial, cohabitating relationships where changing live-in partners is commonplace.
- However, an increasing number of cohabitating couples see themselves as deeply involved, but they also view their relationship as less of a full commitment than that defined by legal marriage.
- Not unlike previous generations, the vast majority of young people today want to marry and have children. However, unlike any past generation, most see cohabitation as a normal, logical "next step" before walking down the aisle or as an alternative to ever marrying.

Considerations about Cohabitating

- It would be easy to assume that with the growth of cohabitation, marriage is becoming an endangered institution. However, it is too early to say this move away from legally binding relationships is a long-term trend or that we are merely seeing the bottom of the marriage cycle and that marriage is on the upswing.
- Cohabitation should no longer be treated as a single social phenomena but, instead, a widely diverse foundation for building an intimate relationship, or at least experimenting with being in one.
- All indications are that cohabitation will be a permanent feature in our society and the basis for a new form of family union. So in light of this reality, the logical response is to work to strengthen the institution of cohabitation—not condemn it.
- Many children of divorce develop the… "I'll not go through what my parents did" mindset and cohabitate instead. Therefore, one could assume that children of cohabitating parents may also develop a similar… "I'll not go through what my parents did" reaction and

marry instead. Therefore, it is possible to forecast that future generations of the children of cohabitation will seek the stability of legal marriage, rejecting the foundation of their parents' cohabitation relationship as just too insecure.

- In this regard, the key is to determine the difference between a cycle and a trend. The current evidence does not verify that cohabitation a long-term, lasting trend or merely part of a multi-generational experiment that will ultimately "fizzle out" due to a loss of interest and lack of perceived benefit.

LESSONS LEARNED

Perhaps you are fully aware of the unfavorable statistics and unsettling facts about cohabitation but think that you can defy the statistics. The main point is that, no matter what brought you to the decision to cohabitate, you may be interested in a new approach to building an intimate live-in relationship. This book details a totally new approach to relationship fitness that will enable you to avoid common problems associated with cohabitation, regardless of your motives, how long your live-in relationship lasts, and what form it ultimately takes. This book offers a new model for building an intimate relationship based on equality, competency, and the realization that it is time for a radical new approach to help young people form, sustain, and strengthen their live-in relationships based on the realities of the 21st century.

If history teaches us anything, it is that none of the existing ways of building significant relationships fully addresses the realities of love and intimacy in the 21st century. As the above statistics show, the rate of cohabitation has risen dramatically while the rate of marriage has steadily declined by nearly 50% in the past 40 years.

While the current rate of divorce reported in 2007 is down among some socioeconomic groups, it is mainly due to the decline in the rate of marriage among other groups. Many people, especially in the 25-34 age range believe there's got to be a better way; and that, in part, is the reason for the continuing rise in the number of people who experiment with cohabitation. They see it as a better or at least different way to establish an intimate relationship.

Therefore, the approach proposed in this book of using winning business strategies to create a winning intimate relationship is also an experiment. While the idea of using business strategies in your intimate relationship may seem a bit too "cut-and-dry" or impersonal, this book is all about intimacy. Nothing destroys a loving relationship and speeds doom for a cohabitating couple faster than power struggles, unresolved conflict, feelings of inequity, and the realization that you both have a very different vision for the future of your relationship.

In addition, this is one of the first books designed to reach men *and* women, which is why it says some very unconventional things about cohabitating and says them in a brand new way. While this book is all about intimacy, it is also a book that a woman does not have to be afraid to give the man in her life. This is not a "touchy-feely" book but more a practical guide to beat the odds and build the fitness of your live-in relationship.

The alternative is to play the odds and take your chances by basing what could be the most important relationship in your life on the traditional relationship model that is failing as much as 50% of the time.

"It is not the strongest of the species that survive, nor the most intelligent, but the one most responsive to change."
—Charles Darwin

The traditional approach to intimate relationships is not inherently good or bad; it is just not responsive to changing conditions and, as a result, it has become outmoded, irrelevant, and simply doesn't work. The traditional foundation for building an intimate relationship is in danger of extinction and simply is not in tune with life in 21st century, with our global economy, unparalleled advances in technology, terrorism anxieties, middle-income stagnation, and unprecedented demands on couples and families. If there were ever a time for a new model for an intimate relationship, it is now.

THE "BUSINESS" MODEL

Making an intimate relationship actually work in today's world means learning from the history of bad judgment in relationships... your own or others. The nature of intimate relationships has changed more in the past few decades than it has in thousands of years... and cohabitation is just one of the many new variations. If you want to build a relationship of the future in the middle of this transformation, you will have to be both a historian and a pioneer.

You must learn from the past and you must courageously go where no one has gone before, using a radically different approach. This new approach for building successful live-in relationships is the "Business" Model, illustrated at the end of this chapter. Just as successful organizations are grounded in established principles and sound strategies, so too can a satisfying cohabitating relationship reap great rewards using the same winning business strategies.

For example, one common business strategy has to do with the importance of having clear expectations about what is anticipated of us on the job. Most employees expect job descriptions that provide clarity, focus, direction, and the specifics of the job, along with some form of documentation that spells out what they will be paid and how they will be evaluated in the future. It would be very frustrating—if not impossible—for the average person to perform his or her job without knowing what was expected and how they would be evaluated.

Yet, frequently, couples move in with each other hoping their relationship will magically fall into place *and* last forever. They do so without the benefit of clear expectations because they lack a job description. Most work/life balance studies show that conflicts about household chores are a common source of conflict for all couples. Worse still, without any agreement as to task requirements or performance expectations, each partner often gives the other daily criticism that only makes matters worse, such as: "I can't believe you spent money on that" or "You're no better than my last roommate" or "Why is the apartment such a mess?"

This book is about using good judgment based on experience to avoid these types of mistakes typical in the traditional relationship model of the past. More importantly, it is about what you can do to be successful and prosper in your relationship by using a totally new model for building relationship fitness. This book does not delve into your past, analyze your parents, or explore all your neuroses—it does not provide psychotherapy. It is one of those rare books for normal people like you and me.

Is This Book Right For You?

Anybody can use this new "Business" Model, even if you have little or no experience actually working in the business world. In addition, concepts and activities in this book can be successfully applied to a budding romance of a newly cohabiting couple or to validate and strengthen a live-in relationship that has lasted years. This book can even provide answers about why previous live-in relationships failed and how your experience of those setbacks can actually improve your judgment in making better relationship choices now.

The "Business" Model is simple and straightforward, but I want to caution you—applying it to your relationship before or after moving in together may not be easy and may even be unsettling at times. But the activities in this book can also be fun and energizing, as you and your partner embark on this process of self-discovery and explore various aspects of your live-in relationship. Enjoy the journey!

This book builds on successful concepts used every day in business that (believe it or not) translate directly to your relationship to increase the honesty, deepen the commitment, and protect the romance while you are cohabitating. There is much to be gained from building a world-class relationship based on winning business strategies!

After reading this book, you will gain a whole new per-spective on how to think about a live-in relationship and its basis, through activities such as discussing the long-term vision of your relationship. With this philosophical framework in mind, you will then get a chance to learn about and work through concrete issues such as setting measurable objectives, funding and branding the relationship, merging "mindstyles," developing job descriptions, giving productive relationship feedback, and conducting relationship meetings and retreats. (In fact, if you want to jump to the chapter on job descriptions and get right into the concrete issues, go ahead. You won't be lost if you are the kind of person who likes to work through practical issues first.) This book will help cohabitating couples:

- Find a clear and common vision for the future state for the relationship
- Develop a set of measurable objectives that define why the relationship exists, where it is headed, and how you will measure success
- Determine attitudes about money and their role in funding a live-in relationship
- Develop a relationship logo and marketing a unified relationship brand
- Learn how to deal with the impact of your different family backgrounds
- Create clear job descriptions that pinpoint each partner's roles and responsibilities
- Design a relationship feedback process complete with tips on regular appraisals
- Learn how to hold regular relationship meetings and retreats where the partners can step back from the relationship and objectively review their progress toward their vision, and then develop new strategies to support their objectives

Maybe you are not business-minded—or perhaps you think that these business-based strategies seem "cut-and-dry." I assure you that the relationship activities and exercises set out in this book are presented in a fun and energizing format. Couples at any stage in their relationship can learn how to create a foundation and structure where romance, authenticity, intimacy, and a sense of true friendship can flourish. This can be accomplished without the problems that typically undermine relationships founded on failed traditional models. If you are still not convinced and do not see the connection between business and live-in relationships, I would like to offer the following for your serious consideration. Most of us would be hard-pressed to describe the specific strategies we use daily or the number of hours spent weekly to maintain and improve our most important intimate relationship.

However, on the other hand, if you are a full-time employee, you spend hundreds of hours a year performing tasks to help your employer maintain and improve his or her bottom line. You are likely performing those tasks for an organization that has some type of business plan that includes a vision and measurable objectives. In addition, you probably have a job description, receive some form of performance feedback, and know something about how the business does compensation planning—and this is all for an employer that you are likely to leave in just a few years.

Don't you think that a relationship that could turn into a lifelong arrangement or a legal marriage deserves the same time, energy, and commitment that you give to your employer? This is what the book is about: applying proven business strategies to achieve a world-class relationship. I assure you that the return on your investment will be well worth the effort.

The "BUSINESS" MODEL

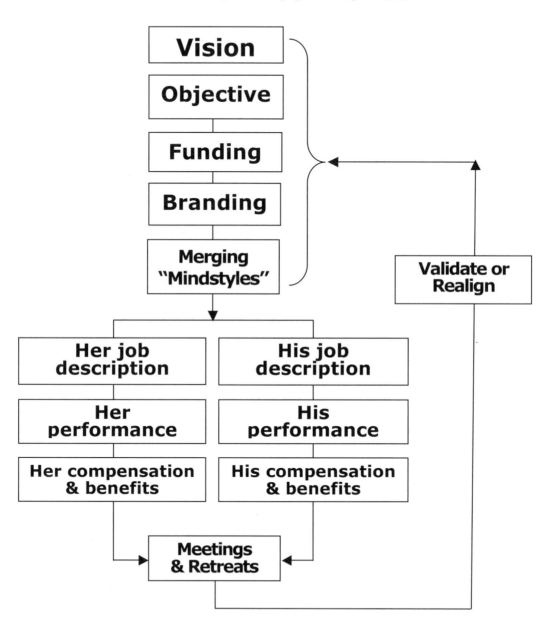

Strategy #1
Creating the Vision
of Your Relationship

"The best way to plan for the future is to create it."
—Peter Drucker, writer, economist, management
consultant, and university professor

Chapter Objectives:

1. Understand the role of a vision statement and its importance in relationship development.
2. Learn how to write a relationship vision statement.
3. Resolve differences in relationship vision statements.
4. Build a unified vision statement for your relationship.

The Ideal State of Your Relationship

It is the rare cohabiting couple who do any long-range planning on how to achieve the relationship they both desire. It is quite amazing how many smart people just assume that somehow once they move in together, things will magically work out. In most cases, these couples simply and blindly "wing it!"

Just like enlightened executives and entrepreneurs who create and continually refine a long-range strategic plan for their business, you and your partner can develop and continually update your own plan for how your relationship will develop and sustain its "profitability." Your vision could have a short time "horizon" or project out over a period of years. Developing this shared vision for your relationship will make it much easier to focus on the more concrete elements of relationships that will be covered in later chapters.

This chapter will begin with writing the vision statement for your relationship: a few words that define your future ideal state of your relationship. But first, let's look at some examples of vision statements that are not about intimate relationships but are simple and easy to grasp, like "a world without hunger, or war, or disease!" Another example is America's Pledge of Allegiance to the Flag…"One nation, under God, indivisible, with liberty and justice for all." As you can see, a vision statement can be basic or bold, idealistic, grand, easy to understand, and sometimes poetic. It should motivate, inspire, and stimulate.

Now, to become a bit more focused, the following demonstrate how some familiar organizations describe their vision.

At **Microsoft**, *we work to help people and businesses throughout the world realize their full potential. As a company, and as individuals, we value:*

- *Integrity and honesty.*
- *Passion for customers, for our partners, and for technology.*
- *Openness and respectfulness.*
- *Taking on big challenges and seeing them through.*
- *Constructive self-criticism, self-improvement, and personal excellence.*
- *Accountability to customers, shareholders, partners, and employees for commitments, results, and quality.*

Special Olympics: *is an unprecedented global movement which, through quality sports training and competition, improves the lives of people with intellectual disabilities and, in turn, the lives of everyone they touch.*

- **Pfizer:** *"We dedicate ourselves to humanity's quest for longer, happier lives through innovation in pharmaceutical, consumer, and animal health products."*

Writing Your Vision Statement

Now, after seeing some examples, you can better understand vision statements and how to write your own—so let's get to work. Your vision statement describes a future ideal state of your relationship. It is often stated in expressive, bold, and poetic terms—a combination of values, ideals, goals, expectations, beliefs, possibilities, and the unique contributions each of you will bring to the relationship throughout your lives.

First, I recommend that you and your partner work on the first draft of your vision statements individually. Begin by writing a version or two that describe, in a few words, your vision for the relationship, before being influenced or biased by what your partner might write. This approach also helps to ensure that one partner does not avoid this challenging task or give in to the other partner's vision in order to "keep the peace."

Remember, this is your life, too!
The success of your relationship is due, in part, to what you
add to the relationship, not what you give up to be in it!

Next, decide on a time and place to discuss your vision statement with your partner. If your partner is not reading this book, then at a minimum, ask him or her to think about it and be prepared to discuss it. Tell your partner how important it is to you to jointly develop a shared vision to help plan for and ensure a successful relationship, however you define it. As is often said in business, "Those who fail to plan, plan to fail," so don't let this be the case with your intimate relationship.

Once you both have made the commitment to this task, block out some time to work on this activity and set a deadline when you will share vision statements in preparation for combining them into a unified vision for the relationship. You'll need time to truly think about your vision of the future. The mental process of creating the vision statement forces you and your partner to stop and wonder, "What is my view of our relationship?

This is where the hard work comes in. Tread slowly and carefully, because this is the first of several activities throughout this book that may be difficult, sometimes unsettling, and yet deeply rewarding. Working to develop a common vision that you and your partner fully support is the first and usually the most difficult hurdle. Early in the process of developing a vision statement, it is likely that you'll think of a vision for you "yourself" rather than for your relationship. Or you may find out that your vision statement appears to be quite different than your partner's vision for the relationship. You may have some major issues to discuss whether you have moved in together yet or not!

That's okay. It is simply part of the process of moving from a single view of the future to one of a couple working in a unified partnership. Imagine your ideal relationship in six months or several years into the future, and envision where you would like your relationship to be, what you and your partner will be doing, what achievements you will have made, what your sense of purpose will be, and so forth. Based on this mental image, begin to write a first draft of a vision statement for your relationship. Keep in mind that it is very unlikely that you will write the ideal statement at first. It is okay to use phases, change the wording, and do lots of editing... just get started, but be sure to use a pencil with a good eraser or be prepared to make many changes in the statement in your computer version.

Getting Started—"Warm-up" Exercises

Exercise # 1—Before you begin writing a vision statement, you might want to do a little pre-work to help you with this task in case nothing immediately comes to mind. You may want to identify some of your core values to incorporate into your vision statement. One way to spot these is to look for tangible items in your life that represent the things you value most. It may be a piece of jewelry you're wearing, an emblem on your key chain, a picture on your computer desktop, or a cherished symbol on the wall.

Typically, these items represent or remind you of something of great value to you... a religious icon, a beloved grandparent, a significant life accomplishment, and so on. A vision statement for your relationship might incorporate these core values, and you may find it easier to begin writing your vision once you have pinpointed tangible items that you treasure.

Exercise # 2—Consider doing a search on the Internet for other examples of vision statements. Go to websites of organizations that you know and trust... consider the web site of your employer (if one exists), or your place of worship, a community hospital, your favorite electronics brand, your alma mater, or even a branch of government. Many examples are readily available, and viewing how others have written vision statements may help you develop a better vision statement for your relationship.

Writing Your Vision Statements

Look at the following examples of two seemingly different vision statements from the same couple. Each partner created her or his statement separately.

His:

In our ideal relationship, we are equal partners but value each other's different approach to life. We will share our daily burdens and successes and pool our financial resources so that we can travel, expand our horizons, and live life to the fullest, free of family and the social burdens of being legally married.

Hers:

My vision for the future ideal state of our relationship is one based on friendship and full of rich meaning and deep love. We each will be devoted to helping the other reach their full potential. We will achieve financial stability and maintain balance in all areas of life together.

You can see that the couple has different priorities, but once the visions are shared and integrated, they may be closer in meaning than they seem. Look for the commonalities in concepts and values, regardless of the words. Are you using synonymous terms that sound different on the surface but are really saying the same basic thing? When you identify core concepts and values within each vision statement, you might find that you are closer to each other than you thought.

Also, don't be concerned if your vision statements sound completely different than these examples. There is no right way to do this, and no pre-determined outcome. The key is to be bold, honest, creative, and future-focused with an emphasis on the ideal state you desire for your relationship.

Combining Your Vision Statements

What you are looking for in this part of the activity can be compared to the lighting of a unity candle at a wedding ceremony. As you may know, it begins with each partner lighting an individual candle. Together, the couple then lights the single unity candle with their individual candles and then extinguishes their separate candles, thus taking two separate flames and making them one. This is a symbol of joining your individual visions into one common vision for the relationship. Even though you are cohabitating and perhaps have no plans for marriage, the unity candle ceremony is a great image to convey the essence of developing a shared vision statement.

A Word on Compromise and Negotiation!

Throughout this book, two types of core personal issues that can lead to potential conflicts in any relationship will be discussed: needs and values. Needs are often common desires or wishes that change over time and tend to be situational, like how you spend your free time, the type of clothes you wear, or how tidy you keep the apartment. Values, on the other hand, are about those long established and difficult-to-change beliefs and ideals like our deeply held views of religion, money, and politics.

Need conflicts can often be resolved through compromise... you can alternate who cleans the bathroom or flip a coin to see whose turn it is to clean it. However, when trying to combine your visions for the future of your relationship into a shared vision, you may run into values conflicts. It is often at this point, when you start to dig deeper into who you are and what you value in the relationship, that you discover new dimensions of your personality and that of your partner. This process of discovery can help you reach new levels of openness that you never imagined possible. At the same time, you may find that you and your partner appear to be far apart on the values that each of you has for the vision of the relationship, and this is where the hard work of negotiating begins OR you realize that living together may not be a good idea.

This process of negotiation is at the heart of the "Business" Model. No matter how long it takes, I urge you to keep talking, discovering, and working toward a common vision for the relationship despite what may at first seem like irreconcilable differences. These discussions may evoke strong emotions and require a concerted effort to stay open and accepting of each other.

Early in my relationship, when we would have what appeared to be a values conflict, I would get very dramatic, which is typical of my negotiating style. I would sound very strong and forceful, but I later found out that Charlotte got scared and reacted by shutting down. Her style was to compromise to achieve peace at any price, so she did not "push back" or "stand her ground," which only frustrated me more because I wanted to negotiate to resolve the issue, not avoid it. Now, as she jokingly states when I get into my dramatic mode, "Oh that's just John!" She is not discounting me, but instead she has learned that is my style, and with a little time, patience and understanding, we always work it through.

In addition, because of working on a vision for your relationship, your worst fear may seem to come true… you and your partner do not appear to be compatible and cohabitating seems to be a bad idea. Certainly, not every relationship is meant to last. Because of poor judgment, you may have moved in with someone that you will later regret. However, I urge you not to jump to conclusions now. Instead, keep exploring by reading about the other strategies described in this book until you make it all the way through. The doubt you might be feeling now may simply be the result of entering a new level of honesty with yourself and intimacy with your partner, so it is only natural to feel anxious and afraid.

Just remember not to "throw in the towel" to avoid anxiety or fear by compromising your values. Doing so may likely mean that you will grow increasingly angry with yourself and your partner as you give up more and more of who you are and what you believe in order to keep the peace... the result of negotiation must be a win-win outcome.

The First Draft of Your Vision Statement!

Use this space to begin a draft of your own vision statement, independent of your partner's.

_____

_____

_____

_____

_____

_____

_____

_____

_____

If it seems too difficult a task to merge your separate visions, set them aside for now and move forward to other strategies that may be more concrete and straightforward for you than this one. A good example of this is where you will write job descriptions for yourself and your partner. You will likely find it easier to talk about more concrete issues such as who does the laundry, who washes the cars, who pays the bills, and who takes care of pets. Don't panic! You can always come back to the vision statement and refine it once you have a better understanding of the more tangible aspects of your life together, or you can move on to Chapter 2 on writing objectives.

Chapter Highlights:
- Translating the benefits of vision statements for organizations directly into improving a new or established live-in relationship
- Aligning long-range values and expectations through a vision statement for the relationship
- Employing a vision statement as the standard by which all else in the relationship is measured.

Strategy #2
Developing Your Relationship's Objectives

"The vision must be followed by the venture. It is not enough to stare up the steps—we must step up the stairs."
—Vance Havne

Chapter Objectives:

1. Understand how to jointly develop relationship objectives.
2. Identify and define the core dimensions of your relationship.
3. Set up measurable objectives for all dimensions of your relationship.

First the What, Now the How

By now, you may have a shared vision of what you and your partner would like your relationship to be in the future or have decided to develop one after reading more of this book. Next, it is time to create a series of measurable objectives that define the specific dimensions of your relationship. Just as many organizations write measurable objectives of what they want to achieve in the area of sales, profit, market share, customer or employee satisfaction, and a wide variety of other outcomes, couples can also work collectively to write objectives that define their relationship outcomes. Typically, objectives can help answer such questions as:

• What are we trying to achieve?

• What are our priorities?

• How do we want to use our resources?

• What measures will we use to determine success?

Unlike the vision statement, relationship objectives are narrow and specific and typically can be grouped into various dimensions that are a part of any relationship. Each dimension helps describe specific areas of activity within your relationship to identify what you both want to achieve in concrete and measurable terms.

Examples of Relationship Dimensions:
1) Family, 2) Financial, 3) Health & Wellness, 4) Intimacy,
5) Spirituality, 6) Leisure, 7) Career

Writing Relationship Objectives

While writing your vision statement was a solitary effort that you then shared and combined as a couple, objectives are best written together from the outset. You and your partner should agree on which dimensions described in this chapter such as financial or career fit your circumstances and are the most important to making your collective vision come true. This exercise will require a good deal of self-awareness, some negotiation, and perhaps a bit of compromise.

After all, if you have an objective to buy a motorcycle and tour the country and your partner is deathly afraid of motorcycles, you might have to settle for touring parts of the country by other means. But the objective is to tour the country, and perhaps you will do some of it in a camper, on a train or by car, or you may do some of it alone on your motorcycle. It's okay to have solitary objectives intermingled with ones you both want to achieve. Single and joint objectives will be discussed in more depth later in this chapter.

Don't worry if some of the dimensions don't apply to you, or if you have trouble deciding what you want in any given dimension, or if you want to add some to the list. Life is fluid and dynamic; aspects of your objectives will be too. Unlike your vision statement, which might have a time "horizon" that might not change over a period of months or years, objectives may be shorter-term and might shift significantly once you achieve certain milestone objectives—such as moving in together, completing college, or changing jobs—and move on to another stage in your lives.

This exercise is likely to be challenging and time-consuming, yet it is not to be hurried. Feel free to break the effort up into multiple meetings or sessions. Start with simply agreeing on the most important dimensions. In subsequent meetings, you can discuss the specific objectives and construct the details.

It is important to note that many of these dimensions are interconnected. For example, if your objective is to travel the country

(Leisure), this objective will have economic implications (Financial). If your objective is to be a manager (Career) for which you need a college degree, this will affect both your continuing education (Life-Long Learning) and investment aspirations (Financial). You may find yourself moving from one dimension to another and back again. That's okay. It is more important to make sure each objective is as measurable, concrete, and specific as you can make it.

The following **S.M.A.R.T.** guidelines, commonly used in business, might help you in writing objectives in each dimension. It is important that your objectives be:

- **Specific**—Objectives are concrete and something you can actually plan for and work toward in a realistic manner.
- **Measurable**—You need to be able to note progress and determine whether you are getting closer to achieving your objective.
- **Achievable**—Objectives you develop for each dimension of the relationship are things that can actually be accomplished.
- **Relevant**—Be sure not to lose touch with reality. Ensure that the objective is tied to the dimension of your relationship that helps to define the reason the relationship exists.
- **Time-bound**—Objectives have a specific and reasonable date by which you plan on accomplishing what you have committed to do, whether it is six months or six years into the future.

Dimensions of a Relationship

Let's begin looking at these different relationship dimensions. Start by asking yourselves, "What would you like to achieve for yourself and your relationship in any or all of the following dimensions?"

1) **Family**—If you're living together but have no children, deciding on if or when you want to marry and/or the number of children you want to have (if any) will be important. Some couples may bring children into the cohabitating relationship from previous relationships. For others, taking care of aging parents will be a major family issue. In the 21st century, the definition of "family" has changed dramatically. Beyond co-habitation, same-sex marriage, foster children, bi-racial families, international adoption, elder care, and stepparents are just a few of the unique facets of what it means to be a contemporary relationship. Be sure to discuss specific objectives that you each have for the family dimension of your relationship.

While much may be beyond your control (like an aging but healthy parent who suddenly suffers a stroke and requires 24-hour attention and care), talking about what you and your partner would likely do if this situation were to arise can go a long way toward preventing a relationship crisis before it ever happens. In addition, discussing these types of issues helps you to learn more about your partner's values and priorities. For example, consider some of the following questions in just a few important areas of this dimension as a way to learn more about each other while developing greater intimacy with your partner:

a. How will you spend the holidays? How do you feel about relatives visiting? How would you deal with a "problematic" sibling or parent who judges us for cohabitating? Do you expect to visit family on vacations?

_____

_____

_____

_____

b. Do you want children? How many? Would you adopt? Should they attend public, private, or religious school? Who is to do the majority of the nurturing and the disciplining?

_____

_____

_____

_____

c. How would you deal with an aging parent? Would you consider having a senile parent move in? How much financial support would you provide a sick or troubled family member?

_____

_____

_____

_____

d. While there are many more issues that can arise in this dimension, don't overlook its importance because it is one area of a committed, intimate relationship that may require skillful negotiations, compromise, or even sacrifice.

2) **Financial**—Have you dreamed of an early retirement? Do you want to start investing? What kind of lifestyle do you hope to achieve in terms of the cars you drive, the home you live in, the clothes you wear, and the material items that you want to own? Be sure to discuss financial objectives with your partner and how you see achieving those objectives. In addition, this area might include how you will finance objectives that have been identified in other dimensions, such as the cost of any further education, travel, and college expenses. At a minimum, this dimension might include an objective about when and how you will develop a financial plan for how to deal with living expenses. Money is often, needlessly, a source of

tension in a cohabitating relationship. However, advanced planning can be one of the most powerfully positive aspects of your relationship. This dimension, too, may easily help you both decide to open a joint checking account, keep your separate accounts, or both.

3) **Health and Wellness**—Do you want to be a tri-athlete, stop smoking, lose weight, or have cosmetic surgery? All of these involve developing specific objectives for the physical aspects of your relationship. Studies verify that healthier couples have happier relationships, and, conversely, that happy couples have a better quality of life—especially men! Be sure to consider mental health as an area where you may want to set some specific objectives. As was stated in the introduction, this book is not meant to provide psychotherapy. It is written for normal people with typical relationship challenges. However, just as with learning to overcome poor health habits, you might need to set an objective in this dimension to address all the phobias or compulsions that you have developed. Unfortunately, some people have suffered trauma in their earlier years that some of us don't just "get over" with the passage of time. If you could simply just "get over" it with the passage of time, senior citizens would be the happiest and mentally healthiest of all generations. In some cases, seeking therapy with a licensed professional is the best way to ensure that you and your relationship are on a sound footing and set up for success. An enlightened business would seek the assistance of an outside expert in a time of need, and your personal life is no different.

4) **Intimacy**—This category can be a challenge since, so often, intimacy is seen as another word for sex and cohabitating,

especially for men who see living together as another way to ensure easy access to a sex partner. In this dimension of the relationship discussion, sex is certainly something to talk about, given the potential differences in sexual appetites of men and women. However, for the sake of discussion, let's agree that there is a difference between sex and intimacy. It is not uncommon for couples to have sexual contact without experiencing intimacy.

The key is to remember that true intimacy at the emotional level is what most partners want in their live-in relationship, but they may not have a clue about how to achieve it. Just watch a few days of commercials or popular television sitcoms and you will see many examples of those simplistic, one-dimensional fantasy relationships.

In such televised depictions, men are preoccupied with sex and see women as nothing but sex objects, and likewise, women are preoccupied with sex and see men as nothing but sex objects. In addition, these television shows often portray men as openly distasteful of anything that hints of emotional vulnerability, while women are often shown as lost, lonely, and emotionally desperate which may be why you are thinking about or have already started your live-in relationship.

In many of these sitcoms, women seem to be paired up with one of those simplistic, one-dimensional men who love themselves, their sports, their beer, or their car more than they love the desperate women who are constantly trying to trap, trick, or get rid of them. Is it any wonder that the popularity of marriage is at a 40-year low and more people are cohabitating than ever?

Remember, having an intimate relationship is not about finding the right person; it is about being the right person. Intimacy is about having deep, loving feelings for your partner and being committed to meeting that person's needs and supporting that person's growth. Many women find intimacy in snuggling, deep conversations, having their partners show sincere interest in their lives, and receiving tokens of their partners' affection (a nice card, flowers, a dinner out). For many men, their partner's showing a genuine interest in their work, their ideas, and their ambitions often conveys intimacy.

5) **Spirituality**—This dimension is about what, if any, religious or spiritual beliefs are important to each of you and how you see religion being integrated into your relationship. If you share the same religion and choose to practice it in the same manner, then this will likely be an easy and brief discussion. However, if there is a difference of opinion about religion or if a chasm exists, now is the time to bring it out and determine your objectives for this dimension of your relationship. In addition, it is important to discuss cohabitating in the context of your religious beliefs since live-in relationships are deemed wrong by all major world religions and most all cultures.

If neither of you is the "religious type," then, at a minimum, consider developing a set of core values that you want to live by... things like integrity, forgiveness, support, trust, compassion. Then develop a code of conduct that will define specific behaviors that reflect these values and how you will address behaviors that do not. This is the time to discuss consequences, what will happen if one partner behaves in a manner that does not reflect agreed upon values. If you jointly claim to value integrity but a partner has an affair, spell out what will be the consequence. Does it mean an immediate end to the relationship and the offending person has to move out, no questions asked? OR, if you also include forgiveness as a core value, does this mean that an affair, while being a complete violation of integrity and trust, may be forgiven depending on the circumstances and following lots of intense communication?

Just as in business, when insubordination or stealing from your employer means immediate termination, it is equally important to discuss consequences for breaking your shared religious morals or core values. This may seem cold or even harsh, but I would argue that this type of clarity would only help to strengthen the intimacy between partners. While much in an intimate relationship may be in shades of gray due to the need for ongoing negotiations and compromise, some things are black and white. As you can see, this dimension of your relationship is likely to bring out some strong reactions and powerful emotions, but don't avoid it since objectives in the spiritual dimension of your relationship will be used throughout other activities in this book and will be referenced later.

Unlike the days when cohabitation was condemned by religion, these days people all too often move in together completely ignoring their religious beliefs or common values. However, in the development of objectives for your relationship, please be thoughtful and deliberate, as your decisions in the spiritual dimension of your relationship will likely affect many, if not all, of the other dimensions. You may not be aware of the ways in which spirituality affects your life now, but that will likely change at some time in the future.

Most important, remember that religious beliefs and core values are not something you can compromise on without taking a toll on the relationship, and communication alone will rarely resolve a values conflict.

6) **Leisure**—In this dimension, you may want to discuss when and how to travel, your hobbies, how to spend time off, your weekend activities, and the pace at which you want to live. Some people would rather have a slower, relaxed pace of life, while others, like me, prefer to be always going, doing, and planning for the next activity.

Are you both the kind of people who like to take a week of vacation and lie on the beach in the islands? Or do you prefer the eco-tourist lifestyle, heading off one year to Machu Picchu, the ancient Inca city high in the Andes Mountains, and off to the rainforests of Thailand the next? Or are you somewhere in between (or split) on how you like to spend your time off? This can often be another great area to negotiate and to practice the all-important skill of compromise.

Besides travel and weekend leisure, you may want to discuss hobbies. Do you like to fish, read, hunt, garden, or do crafts? All of these things require a time commitment and might or might not include your partner.

This is also an opportunity to consider taking up new leisure activities. Perhaps you'd like to take cooking lessons since he does such a great job in the kitchen preparing meals for friends and family. Sometimes collaborating with your partner can spark new interests and hobbies.

7) **Career**—Are you happy with your current position? Is work something that you find extremely rewarding? Does it define who you are, or is it something you do just to pay the bills? Many men are programmed to believe that their work defines their identity while women are programmed to believe that their relationships define their identity. While each belief has its merits, each one also leaves you

vulnerable to the cyclical and unpredictable nature of both work and relationships.

You can begin to see why it is important to plan a lot of time to fully discuss each dimension so that you can define specific objectives that you both would like to accomplish. In your career discussions, be sure to detail how you see your career integrating with your relationship. For most dual-income couples, these are two sides of the same coin; balancing these often-conflicting roles can be the source of chronic tension and anger. How to successfully achieve this balance will be discussed in more detail later in the chapter on job descriptions.

Some people's objectives may be to change careers altogether, while some may want to change their hours or to work from home. Discuss aspirations and dreams openly with each other and really listen to your partner.

Set Clear Objectives

When discussing each life dimension, take time to set clear objectives for what you would like to accomplish, fully hear each other out, and then come up with outcomes that work for you both. If you identify other dimensions that are important to you and your partner, feel free to add them to your list. These objectives, grouped into the various dimensions, are provided only as examples. You may find that several of the dimensions and the objectives listed within them work for you with little or no editing. Or you may find that you need to develop a completely different set of your own dimensions and objectives. Now it is time for your detailed work to begin. It is okay to develop many drafts, change the wording, and do lots of editing... just get started, but be sure to use a pencil with a good eraser or be prepared to make many changes in the objectives on your computer.

SAMPLE DIMENSIONS & OBJECTIVES WORKSHEET	
Dimensions	Objectives
1. Family	1.1 Have a meal together at least 3 times weekly. 1.2 Limit television watching to only those programs we select in advance. 1.3 Develop a relationship with at least one culturally diverse couple each year. 1.4 Always avoid racist, religiously biased, or gender-stereotypical comments. 1.5 Get a small-breed dog in the next 2 years. 1.6 Decide whether to get married or have children in the next 3 years.
2. Financial	2.1 Consolidate our checking accounts within the next 3 months. 2.2 Register our cars in both our names within 1 month. 2.3 Evaluate our need for life insurance in 1 year. 2.4 Donate 5% of our net income on an annual basis. 2.5 Develop a cash rainy-day fund equal to 2 months of living expenses within the next year. 2.6 Reduce our credit card debt by 50%.
3. Health & Wellness	3.1 Learn Hatha Yoga by the end of this year. 3.2 Walk together for at least 30 minutes twice weekly. 3.3 Reduce caffeine consumption to 2 cups of coffee—only in the morning. 3.4 Begin strength training at the gym within 6 months. 3.5 Attend a smoking-cessation class by the end of this year.
4. Intimacy	4.1 Go out on a "date" at least 2 times each month. 4.2 Commit to never going to sleep before discussing something that might be troubling us. 4.3 Do something romantic and unexpected at least once monthly. 4.4 Learn how to give a massage to each other within a year. 4.5 Read a relationship article or book together at least twice a year. 4.6 Alternate who initiates sexual relations.

SAMPLE DIMENSIONS & OBJECTIVES WORKSHEET	
Dimensions	Objectives
5. Spirituality	5.1 Find a new congregation within 5 miles of our new home by the end of the year. 5.2 Visit the Holy Lands before getting married. 5.3 Read the Bible weekly. 5.4 Attend religious services at least twice monthly. 5.5 Take a class in spirituality within a year.
6. Leisure	6.1 Take a weekend vacation at least twice a year. 6.2 Take one international vacation within 3 years. 6.3 Enter 1 tri-athlete event within a year. 6.5 Begin planning a how will we deal with the holidays before the end of summer. 6.6 Take dance lessons within 12 months. 6.7 Develop a MySpace site within 3 months.
7. Career	7.1 Become department manager by the time I reach 30. 7.2 Accept a relocation offer only if we both agree it is best. 7.3 Develop our own online business within 1 year. 7.4 Confer with my employer about my career options once we move in together. 7.5 Complete a B.A. in business by the time I reach 30. 7.6 Read at least 1 career-related book a month. 7.7 Become proficient with one new software application every 6 months.

If you are a fan of developing lists and doing lots of detailed planning, you can drill down even deeper on your own with each objective. Consider the following as an example of the level of detail that might be helpful for you and your partner to ensure that you achieve what you set out to accomplish. It can feel very satisfying to come up with such a detailed roadmap to certain dimensions of your life and then actually achieving your objective.

Objective 7.7 – Complete a college degree in business by the time I'm 30.			
Action Step	**Interim dates**	**Time/ Resources**	**Outcome/ Results**
7.1.1 Apply for the entrance exam	April 10	3 hrs.	accepted
7.1.2 Apply for tuition supplement at work	May 25	2 hrs.	approval
7.1.3 Research top B.A. programs in the area	May-July	12 hrs.	prioritized list
7.1.4 Prepare for the entrance exam	July–Aug.	30-50 hrs.	1200+ score
7.1.5 Apply to top 2 B.A. programs	Aug.–Oct.	10-25 hrs.	submission
7.1.6 Research & determine tuition budget	June–Aug.	5-10 hrs.	file
7.1.7 Visit each campus	Oct.–Dec.	3 days	select program
7.1.8 Prepare for enrollment	Jan. or Sept.	1 day	begin classes

Personal expanded objectives:

Objective:			
Action Step	**Interim dates**	**Time/ Resources**	**Outcome/ Results**

By now, you might have built a good basis for the philosophical foundation of your relationship by completing a joint vision statement (it is okay if you have tabled the vision statement activity until later). However, if nothing else, you might now have a good start on developing a detailed set of S.M.A.R.T. objectives in each of the relationship dimensions.

You are almost ready to move on to the next step necessary to fulfill your relationship's vision and objectives… writing a job description for each partner to determine who will be responsible for each objective in every dimension. For example, if you've identified a number of financial objectives, you will need to decide if you are going to open a joint checking account, who will pay the bills, and who will monitor the finances to make sure they are meeting your stated objectives. In addition, you need to decide what, if any, major financial decisions must be made like buying a new TV. Your job descriptions will need to answer these questions.

Before you move on to writing job descriptions, there are other prerequisite topics that you need to address in the next chapters on funding the relationship, creating a "brand" image for your relationship, and dealing with merging personal "mindstyles."

However, before moving on, the following is a list of some questions that are designed to build intimacy. First, give them some thought and write down or think about your answers. Then, maybe you'll want to discuss one, two, or all of your answers with your partner. Whether responses to these questions are kept private or shared, these questions are good "food for thought" and typically increase emotional intimacy.

20 Questions to Build Intimacy!	Your Answers!
1. What is your favorite term of endearment (honey, sweetie, etc.)?	
2. What do you like most about living together? Least?	
3. When you pray; what do you pray for?	
4. What is your biggest fear about asserting yourself with me? With others?	
5. What is one habit I have that you wish I would change?	
6. What would you like to be doing when you are 25, 30, or 40?	
7. Do you think God has a physical form? If so, what is it?	
8. Do you swear when you are not around me; if so, what causes you to do it?	
9. Do you ever think about leaving me? What would cause you to take that action?	
10. Do you fear that I would ever leave you? For what reason?	

20 Questions to Build Intimacy!	Your Answers!
11. Do you ever think that our moving in together was a mistake?	
12. What are you most proud of in our relationship?	
13. What is one material possession you do not have but wish you did?	
14. What do you think happens when we die?	
15. What scares you most about your relationship with me?	
16. Have you ever thought about having an affair? Why?	
17. What is your biggest financial worry?	
18. Where is your favorite place to make love?	
19. When is your favorite time of day?	
20. What do you fear most about being more emotionally intimate with me?	

Relationship Dimensions & Objectives Setting Worksheet

Use the following form to build a list of the various dimensions of your relationship and then write S.M.A.R.T. objectives for each dimension.

Dimensions	Objectives

Chapter Highlights:

- Discussing your shared desires and priorities as a couple
- Deciding what life dimensions best fit your life together
- Creating a shared set of S.M.A.R.T. objectives that work in conjunction with your vision statement

Strategy #3
Funding the Partnership Venture

"Disposable income is a good thing."

—Richard Bloodworth, my very best friend

Chapter Objectives:

1. Determine your attitudes about money and how it affects your relationship.

2. Understand how your history with money affects your own as well as your partner's financial objectives as adults.

3. Discuss ways to negotiate, compromise, or change things for the better when it comes to dealing with money in your relationship.

Money might not buy happiness, but it can sure expand your range of choices while living together and waiting for happiness to arrive. In addition, it can, unfortunately, increase the likelihood of conflicts over how to spend it. Few things in our lives bring out stronger emotional reactions than how we feel about money and, as you know, a couple may have very different attitudes about it. The way we handle money and our view of its role in a relationship usually comes from the way we were raised and how our parents dealt with money.

How Do You Feel About Money?

Since money is such a significant problem in relationships, I feel it needs greater emphasis. But before we go any further, here's my disclaimer. This chapter is not about investments, retirement planning, the best income tax software, or which financial advisor to choose. Instead, this chapter is about funding the vision for your relationship, ensuring the resources are there to achieve your objectives, and discovering your attitudes that affect how each of you deals with money.

Unfortunately, if you and your partner have differing attitudes toward money, you will need to have some clarifying conversations in search of common ground in funding your relationship. Differences over money are not something that you can simply agree to disagree on.

First, it's important to understand how you feel about money. Is it something you hoard and fear spending, or do you spend every cent you make, or are you somewhere in between? What is your relationship with money? Historically, what attitudes toward money and wealth did you grow up with, and do you still feel this way now?

Do you believe that the man should make more money than the woman and, if so, why? Do you connect your self-worth to the size of your paycheck?

Do you think that if you live together, all expenses should be split 50/50? Or have you been burned in the past so you are not ready to combine finances? Do you think keeping separate checking accounts is fair? Who do you think should buy dinner when you go out, now that you are living together?

After you figure out how you feel about money, listen to what your partner has to say about money too. Be honest and talk about it with each other. If you've never thought about it before, you may be amazed at what you can learn about yourself and your partner.

Family Myths

It is also helpful to think about your parents' attitudes and how these attitudes affected their marriage. You'll most likely find a pattern there for why you feel a certain way toward money and all that it can symbolize. In fact, I'm sure if you looked at how their parents (your grandparents) handled money, you'd find a similar pattern there too.

For example, my partner grew up in a household where no one talked about money, though the family was financially well off. Her father supplemented spending time with her and her siblings by spending money on them. For her family, money was secretive and something that the man of the house was expected to handle. Her father often gave her money while simultaneously saying, "Do you think money grows on trees?" She knew he worked hard for the family's income, but she had no concept of money and wealth management. So, you can imagine how surprised she was when I asked her to take over the management of our personal checking account and bookkeeping software. She now manages the joint checkbook using financial software, routinely making electronic fund transfers and paying bills online. Since she spends a majority of the money in the household, it is logical for her to manage it on a day-to-day basis. She gets to see how much money comes in and how much money goes out. Her relationship to money has completely transformed her attitudes about it, as well as changed the face of what our partnership means to her. She used to think that it was rude to ask about money, and I assumed that she did not care about our finances. Now, however, money is no longer a secretive topic or a substitute for something else. It simply sustains our lifestyle. She manages money in an efficient and frugal manner and is a great bargain shopper, and I never worry about her wasting or mismanaging our financial resources.

As for me, I grew up in a home where there never seemed to be enough money. The subject of money and its absence in my family brought about feelings of anxiety. My father did not bring in a steady income. My mother's job sustained us, but we all knew that things were tight.

I was the kind of kid who saved every penny. I even made money by digging through dumpsters at the local bike shop for spare parts to make bicycles. I sold them to the kids in the neighborhood for $5, and I rarely spent a penny of it. As an adult, I am still frugal, yet I've learned to overcome many of those early uncomfortable feelings about money through a faith-based money management class. This class gave me a new sense of peace about money and material goods and the proper stewardship of both.

Dealing with Our Attitudes

We also get our attitudes from various places other than family, such as education, media, peers, society, and, in particular, religion. Often religion and wealth are seen as opposites, and certain uninformed zealots like to tell us "money is the root of all evil." For the sake of this discussion about money, religion, and funding your marital vision, it is important to note that the actual verse is, *The love of money is the root of all evil."* (1 Timothy 6:10) Big difference! Having money and enjoying your life does not necessarily lead to evil or sin— only a greedy, unnatural focus on money and materialism leads there. God never expected people to be broke! Love your partner, not your money.

Many of us in a long-term relationship will have psycho-logical issues to work out with regard to money so that it won't hurt our relationship. Use the questions at the end of this chapter to help identify your attitudes about money. Share your thoughts on the differences and/or similarities in your attitudes about money, material goods, and savings.

Many couples cohabitate because they get caught in the trap of "needing" the two incomes because it buys them the lifestyle they think makes them happy or that they feel pressured to create. But this may backfire, since the couple ends up resenting work because they spend so much time apart trying to earn the money to be able to enjoy time together... get the paradox? The one thing the couple wants to do is to have a good life and share time together—yet they are robbed of it because they are in the dual-income trap. More money, obviously, doesn't always make for more happiness. From my perspective, money buys choices and freedom from certain burdens—nothing more. In the pressure of a business or live-in relationship, money often becomes the focus of the power struggles I mentioned earlier in this chapter. When there's a financial power struggle, money becomes a tool for manipulation—warped into something more than it is.

Understand where you and your partner's attitudes about money come from and discuss ways to negotiate, compromise, or change things for the better. To live together, yet not fight about money, is such a glorious luxury in today's society. Be on the cutting edge and work to free your relationship of one of the most common power struggles that can damage or destroy even the most loving relationship! While cohabitating, financial serenity is possible with your current income… it's just that you both might have some background work to do in order to actually believe that and truly feel that way.

Money & Attitudes Questions		
Considerations	What did you learn about money? Was it positive or negative? Why?	How can this lesson benefit your relationship?
1. What role did money play in your life as a child?		
2. How did your parents feel about money?		
3. How did your parents' attitudes about money affect you?		
4. Have you or someone you've known used money to manipulate or dominate? Why? What was the result?		
5. What role does money play in your life now?		
6. How much is your self-concept tied to your income?		
7. What do you or will you teach your children about money?		
8. Have you ever spent money to cope with an emotionally upsetting situation? When? What was the outcome?		
9. Do you think men should make more money than women and why?		
10. Should we share one bank account or keep them separate?		

Chapter Highlights:

- Understanding how you feel about money and how it affects your relationship
- Looking at how your upbringing and your family's attitudes about money plays into your own attitudes about it
- Negotiating and compromising with your partner to ensure that you share productive attitudes about money as you fund your relationship vision and work to achieve your common objectives

Strategy #4
Branding and Marketing
Your Relationship

"You can't blow an uncertain trumpet."
—Fr. Theodore Hesburgh,
Former President, University of Notre Dame

Chapter Objectives:

1. Learn what a relationship brand is and why it is important.
2. Have fun finding the brand logo or symbol that you both can agree on.
3. Discover how and why to market your relationship brand to family and friends.

Who "We" Are!

Relationships have two faces: a private one and a public one. It is not uncommon for those faces to be different and even divisive, but it is unfortunate. The bigger the gap between the two faces, the bigger the risks to the long-term sustainability of the relationship. While there are certain aspects of any live-in relationship that are best kept private, it is critical that both the internal and external faces of the relationship be based on a common vision and objectives that collectively identify the relationship "brand."

The biggest benefit of branding and marketing your relationship is that it ensures that whenever you or your partner describe the relationship to others, you are both drawing from the same vision, values, and attitudes about the relationship. This strengthens the psychological bond, fortifies the emotional commitment, and adds to the level of intimacy each of you feels toward the other.

One of the biggest problems for cohabitating couples occurs when they are not unified in their relationship "brand," so that they seem to be describing two very different relationships. In this chapter, we will discuss developing a unified "brand" for your relationship and the importance of consistently marketing it to your family and friends who may be sitting in judgment or even condemnation of your "living in sin!"

A critical element for success in any business is for it to have a very clear sense of its identity—what it stands for, the emotional relationship it hopes to establish with its customers—and an ability to market that sense of identity to the world. This means going beyond the company's vision and objectives to formulate a brand that fits the business philosophically and typically conjures up an emotional response and connection for the customer.

Nike, Coke, Apple, Mercedes, and Harley-Davidson are some of the most recognized brands in the world. When you see any of these company logos, they cause an immediate emotional response and, whether your reaction is positive or negative, you feel it right away. You get a clear sense of what Mercedes and Apple stand for from the marketing of those logos and the concepts of who they are as a company. A brand is simply a symbol of that identity—a reminder of your emotional relationship with the company behind the logo.

An example from my consulting work with a law firm provides insight into the role and significance of relationship branding. A colleague and I were helping a law firm build a strategic plan that included a marketing program. These were personal injury lawyers who had a hard time breaking out of the stereotypical image of ambulance chasers. My colleague was a brand specialist, and he gave the partners of the firm an assignment using magazines and newspapers, scissors, some glue, and poster board. He told them to cut out the images that portrayed what they did not want to be, as well as the images of what they did want to be as a firm. It ended up being a fascinating exercise for them. They took those "anti-images" (an ad with an overweight guy in a Hawaiian shirt holding a martini and smoking a big cigar, and surrounded by voluptuous women in bikinis around a hotel pool in Las Vegas) and glued them onto one big piece of poster board.

On the other poster board was, among other more positive images, a picture of a lion's head with a strong and confident look on its face, which the partners saw as reflecting integrity and the courage to do battle if need be. That lion's head ended up as a symbol of their brand, and it became the logo for the firm. The firm uses these poster board images of what they do and do not want to be to make sure they are still on the right path. That is an example of a brand logo: a symbol that conjures up emotions, values, or beliefs of what you stand for and want others to know about your brand.

Branding a relationship means that you both work to find a symbol, a logo, that represents what you, the partners, see as the essence of your relationship. As you might have guessed, I'm going to ask you to do the same exercise as the attorneys in the law firm. Make it a fun event some evening, and while it may seem silly at first, it can be a powerful way to create a brand logo of who you are as a cohabitating couple. Work together to go through magazines, newspapers, or the Internet to collect images of what your relationship is and what it is not.

Try to agree on one or two images that may work in unison with each other. If you really do not agree on an image, take more time to discuss it. Or, if you find nothing in any of these sources, maybe one of you could design a new image encompassing both of your ideas. It can even be a newly created symbol, but just make sure that the symbol gives both of you a sense of meaning and reminds you of the essence of your relationship whenever you see it. In addition, even consider identifying a song that supports your brand and will further identify your relationship. Intel, the giant computer microchip maker, has done a great job of linking a familiar four-part tone in all their commercials to their brand. Anytime we hear the familiar tone in a commercial, most of us will immediately think of Intel. Beethoven's Ode to Joy was played at our wedding, and our son and daughter-in-law had it played for us as we walked down the aisle at their wedding.

Whenever Charlotte or I hear that music, we have a rush of warm emotions.

Keep the poster boards, unified symbol, or a version of the song so you can revisit these images at your annual retreat that will be discussed later, and make sure that you, too, use your brand to stay on the path to a world-class relationship.

Marketing Your Relationship's Brand

So, you've found or created a brand logo that represents who you are as a couple. Now, it is time to let others know what your relationship is all about. In the business world, it is about marketing your brand. But why do you need to market something so intimate to the people in your lives, you ask? First, let's take a brief look at why businesses market their brand images.

Companies typically market to sell more products and services. In addition, companies market their brand for other reasons: they market to keep loyal customers, to stay ahead of their competition, to sell more to existing customers, to attract employees, and even to attract other organizations who want to work in partnership with them. In other words, companies need stakeholders, partners, and friends who believe in what they do and who want to associate with them.

In a relationship, while you have each other, it is also normal and healthy to spend time with family and friends. Even though you clearly have no product or service to sell, one key benefit of developing and marketing your relationship brand is that you are likely to attract other like-minded couples. This both reinforces the relationship that you have and helps you to learn from the relationships of others by "benchmarking" your relationship with those around you.

This simply means that you use the relationships of others as a point of reference to determine the health of your relationship. It is hard enough to find good examples of positive and productive relationships anywhere in our society. So anytime that you can learn the "best practices" of other healthy couples through comparative benchmarking, you enhance the return on your investment in developing and marketing your relationship brand.

If you and your partner are ever in a social situation with other couples and you find yourself uncomfortable with the nature of the interactions and behavior of other couples, be sure to discuss your emotional reaction later in private. It is not that you will gossip about or judge others; instead, it is an excellent opportunity to do comparative benchmarking by recognizing what you do or don't want in your relationship. On the other hand, perhaps you may feel a bit envious because you see something modeled by another couple that you would like to have more of in your relationship. Be sure to talk about it as well and consider it a great opportunity to learn how to strengthen your relationship by learning from the best practices modeled by other couples.

There's another reason to do relationship brand marketing. It is my belief that if you don't give people a positive perception of who you are as a couple, they will make one up for themselves and categorize you in a way that might be negative and/or unwanted. This will be especially true for a couple who are "only" living together. As mentioned, all relationships have different faces, and people see only the face that you show them. Sometimes the opinions others form about you as a couple can be harmful to your relationship.

Take, for example, the stereotypical situation with the parents. Do you ever go to dinner with your or your partner's parents, and one of them takes your partner's side on every issue and you feel constant pressure to get married? Or worse, they pick on your partner for cohabitating and never give him or her any support? Why is that? It is possibly because the parents don't see you as a cohesive couple with a united front and are secretly or openly trying to drive you apart. In fact, these episodes with the parents may cause you to fight all the way home, becoming exactly as the relatives see you: divided against each other. It can be a self-fulfilling prophecy when people emphasize a certain image of you, and that certainly holds true for a couple too. If your friends take you and your partner's playful banter as true fighting, they may egg you on at every gathering or party, which can escalate to real arguments that in time may start to weaken your relationship, so they can feel justified in their judgment of your "sinful" relationship.

Purposely marketing a unified brand of who you are as a couple will let the people you spend time with know the brand of your relationship and how you want to be viewed. Now, this doesn't mean that you can't be yourselves and continue that playful banter. But once in a while, one of you can say something like, "One thing I love about Gina is that she likes to tease me as much as I love to tease her. We are both very playful that way."

I'm not suggesting you and your partner be people you are not. It's quite the opposite. I am asking you to know who you are as a couple—your brand—and to market it appropriately as a key strategy toward continually strengthening your live-in relationship. Nike, Coke and McDonalds continually market their brands to reinforce the image of who they are and what they stand for. You and your partner should continually market your brand to ensure those around you know what you stand for as a couple and that you are not living together simply because your relationship is too shallow to support something more permanent.

The United Front

Parents often talk about the importance of presenting a united front when dealing with their children. Of course, this doesn't mean you are clones of one another, but it does mean you both set the rules and enforce them with similar, agreed-upon methods. If parents don't form a united front, the kids may see the differences as vulnerabilities and use them against the parents. It's no different with friends and family.

Pick out those qualities or values from your brand that you most want to put forth. No matter what your partner says to other people about you, always make sure that they know you support each other. No matter what your partner forgets to do or how frustrated you or others can get, let others know you are with your partner all the way. While venting your irritation about your partner to a close friend, it's a good idea to add something like, "Oh well, it's a good thing we share the same vision and values; it helps me get past the occasional little disagreements quickly." Live the brand!

In business, it's sometimes mentioned that you should have an "elevator speech" for what you do—meaning a quick description of what you do for a living that you can give in just a few moments. When you meet someone on an elevator who says, "What do you do for XYZ Corporation?" it's good to have a well-thought-out and crisp answer ready. The same goes for your relationship. When someone asks, "So you've been living together for two years now, huh? How's it going?" It's good to have a genuine answer that reaffirms your feelings about the relationship, "I've found my best friend and moved in with him, and we just keep getting better every day!" It is like having a tag line for your relationship just like the corporate brands.

As a counterbalance to the chronically high failure rate of intimate relationships, consider becoming much more purposeful in the care and nurturing of the most important relationship in your life. Discovering or developing your authentic relationship brand and marketing it consistently can be a powerful tool to help keep you both well connected... and make the relationship world-class regardless of whether you are getting married or plan to live together forever.

This is a chance for you to feel more in charge of your relationship's destiny. To take relationship brand marketing one step further, consider creating your own MySpace page since it is so easy to do. It's the place where you post pictures or notices of your partnership or planned events and market your brand to the world. Write quarterly e-newsletters to all of your family and friends that reinforce the brand images of who you are as a couple. Building a world-class relationship means you need to do things differently to make your relationship successful. Developing and marketing a relationship brand is certainly outside-the-box thinking! Besides, it will really surprise all those critics who are just waiting for your relationship to fall apart.

Steps to developing a relationship brand
1. Go through magazines, newspapers, or the Internet together to find pictures, symbols, or images of what your relationship *is* and what it *is not*. Try to agree on one or two images that may work in

unison. Cut out or print out your images and paste them on a poster board.

2. If you find nothing in any of those sources, maybe one of you could design a new image encompassing both of your ideas. Just make sure that your newly created symbol gives both of you a sense of meaning and reminds you of the essence of your relationship whenever you see it.

3. In addition, consider identifying a song that supports your brand and will further symbolize your relationship. Even consider creating your own online presence to post pictures or notices about the relationship or planned events, and to market your brand to the world. Write quarterly e-newsletters to all of your family and friends that reinforce the brand images of who you are as a couple.

4. Keep the poster board of symbols, or a version of the song or website, so you can revisit these at your annual retreat, which will be discussed later in this book.

5. Consider writing a relationship "tagline" just like major corporations—just a few genuine words that reaffirm your feelings about the relationship. Example: "I've found my best friend, moved in with him, and we just keep getting better every day!"

Chapter Highlights:

• Understanding what a relationship brand is, why you need one, and how to live the brand

• Identifying and agreeing on your specific relationship brand image, symbol, or song

• Using the brand to market who you are as a couple to your family and friends

Strategy #5

Merging Your "Mindstyles!"

"Growth is the only evidence of life."

—Cardinal John Henry Newman

Chapter Objectives:

1. Explore the significant differences between what it means to be a family today compared to a family in the past.

2. Understand mergers and acquisitions in the context of couples and families.

3. Blend family and life cultures based on differing family histories.

4. Learn how to deal with the consequences of being in a blended family situation without losing your identity or uniqueness for the sake of the relationship.

To Merge or Not?

Typically, when two companies merge, the hope is that the whole will be greater than the sum of the parts. Ideally, businesses unite to create a whole new organization with a fresh identity and culture. This hoped for "new identity" is an idealized state that is also the goal when cohabitating. Being happily unmarried means creating a new partnership that allows each participant to gain, grow, and benefit—in other words, to profit from the union by bringing together two people to form a more valuable and worthy partnership.

In the context of intimate relationships, a merger is based on an equal pairing of partners who have decided to move in together to form a new entity in the form of a cohabitating couple. You may also gain a larger family system that includes stepchildren, your partner's parents, quasi in-laws who, for better or worse, come as part of the deal.

The Challenges of Merging

As an organizational development consultant, I am sometimes hired to help manage the change that occurs during the transition that results from a merger or acquisition. In a lot of ways, this work is similar to what I did as a marriage counselor years ago when couples were remarrying. As a counselor then and as a consultant now, my job is to help successfully blend the previously separate and sometimes quite different cultures into a new enterprise that achieves what both parties envisioned when they decided to join forces.

When dealing with a merger, there are two essential dimensions in a business that need to be considered. The first element is the structural dimension, which includes the physical elements of the business, systems, processes, organizational structure, workforce, facilities, inventory, and so on. During most mergers and acquisitions, the focus is on the structural dimension—deciding which plants to close, what HR system is the most effective, consolidating warehouse operations, laying off staff, and so on. What gets missed is the cultural dimension, which is far more important for success and involves the less visible, yet very powerful, aspects of operations, such as the patterns of communication, company values, levels of teamwork, organizational history, workload, attitudes of workers, and so on. As consultants, we go in and research the different cultures by conducting staff interviews, surveys, and focus groups to determine what the cultures are like and what the organizations' "change readiness" capabilities are.

A business merger is a challenging undertaking, and unfortunately in many cases, the whole becomes less than the sum of the parts if both the structural and cultural dimensions are not proactively addressed. The same can be said of an intimate live-in relationship. It can be a very difficult since you'll need to integrate the structural components of what both parties bring to the relationship, such as financial resources, automobiles, furniture, and other possessions. But you also have to integrate the cultural dimension, such as visions, objectives, and values that each of you brings to the relationship.

Beyond these key factors, you will need to successfully integrate patterns of communication, negotiation styles, problem solving skills, and stress-coping mechanisms. If you did not already include learning new interpersonal skills to strengthen your relationship while developing your objectives, consider going back to the objective-setting activity.

Suppose for a moment that you fall in love with a man who has two sons from a previous marriage and an ailing parent. Do you run away screaming, "It can't be done," which is certainly a viable option, or do you roll up your sleeves and accept the challenge of a very tough merger? Remember that nothing worthwhile is ever easy.

Merging Your "Mindstyles"

Mind•style, n.: "The beliefs, attitudes, values, and behavior that characterizes an individual and their unique life experiences."

One of the most common and difficult forms of merging "mindstyles" is when one or both partners of the cohabitating couple are raising children from a previous relationship. This is true whether one of the partners has custody of the child or children or only visitation rights. Parenting in this type of arrangement is not necessarily more difficult than parenting in general, but it can include some very unique challenges. The potential conflicts that might arise between partners with regard to parenting are likely to be values conflicts over things like disciplining children or needs conflicts over things like children's bedtime.

As described earlier in the discussion on negotiation, value conflicts are much more difficult to address and are rarely resolved by compromising on your standards of discipline, while a conflict of needs over bedtime, for example, may be easy to resolve through compromise. The key to successfully blending "mindstyles" is to ensure that you and your partner establish a common vision that includes the children, establish clear objectives regarding how the children will be raised, and determine your parenting roles and responsibilities as part of writing your job descriptions.

Gaining a Partner, Not Losing Yourself

No one purposely moves in with someone to lose "who they are." Neither you nor your partner wants to lose your respective personal identities, beliefs, or values when you cohabitate. However, cohabitation may mean that roles will change, priorities may shift, and parental attention may be diverted to the new live-in partner. The overarching goal here is to keep the best of each person's personal "mindstyle." That's why many of the exercises in this book are meant to help you strengthen who you are as an individual while eliminating barriers in your relationship by discussing, not avoiding, difficult issues. Growing your relationship, like growing a business, takes forethought and courage to focus on and resolve what is most contentious, so that the love and intimacy can flourish with fewer roadblocks.

So how do you measure beliefs, customs, practices, and behavior that are vague? In a relationship, it is often easy to identify examples of each partner's "mindstyle." How were your separate residences decorated, what types of music or food do you each prefer, what is your favorite television show, or how do you like to spend time socializing with friends? One simple but powerful example of "mindstyle" that you each bring to the relationship is how your family celebrates holidays.

Major holidays can be the source of great tension for many cohabitating couples if there is a significant difference in their families and the expectations they bring to the relationship about how to celebrate these events. Perhaps one partner grew up in a large, extended family that never missed the chance to gather as a family. Holidays throughout the year were cherished opportunities to get together and talk, laugh, cry, eat, and generally have fun. On the other hand, if the other partner was an only child raised by a depressed mother and alcoholic father, holidays may have been dreaded. Obviously, in this case, as a live-in couple it is easy to pick how you want to spend holidays in your new relationship.

The key is to realize that differing "mindstyles" are part of the unique traditions each of you brings to the new partnership. However, it is essential that you spend time talking about the places where there are significant differences in your respective "mindstyles" to avoid problems even before they arise. Identify traditions from each of your "mindstyles" that you want to integrate into the new partnership or decide on new traditions that you want to establish.

Just be sure to address the issues of "mindstyles" before your mother calls and says, "You will be coming to our house for the holidays, won't you?" If you don't start your own traditions around the holidays, you may find yourself going to multiple holiday dinners in an attempt to please everyone. Yet, no one ends up happy, you resent the process as you hurry around town pretending to be hungry at each stop, and there is little to give thanks for except that the day is over. This is especially difficult if you both come from big families who love to gather and celebrate holidays. Again, negotiations and compromise are the keys to navigating this touchy situation in an attempt to find a solution that is a win-win.

The challenge is to learn what you want the "mindstyles" of your combined relationship to be... to progress from what it is now and to what you want it to be. This may mean more frank discussions, lots of negotiating, better planning and strategies, redoing your vision or objectives, and so on.

Below are just a few questions that you may want to consider to help you better navigate the merger process before you hit an unplanned obstacle.

1. What possessions are you not willing to give up when we live together?

_____

_____

2. How would you respond to a sibling or relative who needed to borrow money?

_____

_____

3. What holidays are most important to you? How do you like to celebrate them?

_____

4. How much, if any, contact will you likely have with your ex-spouse, partner?

_____

_____

5. How should we deal with disciplining our children from a previous relationship?

_____

_____

6. How do you feel about having friends of the opposite / same sex?

_____

_____

The next chapter deals with writing detailed job descriptions that encompass your new merged status. Having solved the problems that come with mergers will enable you to tackle more concrete elements of the relationship in chapters to come.

Chapter Highlights:
- Figuring out whether you are merging different "mindstyles" into one cohesive yet different couple
- Recognizing the challenges of intimate relationships and blended families in today's times
- Gaining an understanding of what it takes to integrate a blended family and combine "mindstyles"

Strategy #6

Job Descriptions for Couples

Who Does What and How!

"We have the Bill of Rights.
What we need is a Bill of Responsibilities."
—Bill Maher, comedy talk show host

Chapter Objectives:

1. Understand the importance of having clear and attainable job descriptions for both you and your partner.

2. Learn how to divide (and conquer) tasks and write detailed job descriptions for both of you.

Dishes, Duties, and Daily Chores

Taking a business approach to cohabiting helps you protect the romance in your relationship. By taking away the things that typically erode these wonderful feelings, such as stress and resentment over household tasks, common disagreements, or financial burdens, you can focus on the fun and contentment of life. As unromantic and analytical as it may seem, the strategies in this book are meant to help you identify and overcome the barriers to a successful relationship to ensure that you will have more emotional space to enjoy each other and operate like a team or true partnership. If you follow the steps outlined, the hard part will already be resolved!

One of the most important things you can do in a business or relationship of any sort is to have clear and attainable job descriptions for everyone involved. A job description allows you to have good role clarity as well as a clear understanding of how you are expected to perform your job. Both partners must contribute to a relationship; and the things you do on a daily basis, as part of your job description, make up this contribution.

In the business world, every employee, from the mail clerk to the CEO, has a job description, either in writing or at least based on the historical behavior of whoever did that job before them. Some job descriptions may not be formalized, but there's at least a list of tasks and responsibilities that are provided or discussed. Otherwise, a company would not work very efficiently, if at all. Managers and supervisors use these lists of tasks to analyze your performance and to recognize and compensate you.

It is for these very reasons that I think it makes perfect sense for you and your partner to purposefully write job descriptions to define what each of you will do daily to maintain the relationship.

Still not convinced? Do you think your partner already has a clear idea of what you expect of him? Don't be so sure.

Work/life balance studies show that one of the most common sources of conflict between couples is over household chores. This issue all too often becomes a chronic battlefield and it takes all the kindness and caring out of an intimate relationship. A real preventive measure against this conflict is to develop a complete listing of all the recurring tasks that must be accomplished to run your relationship on a daily basis—and then work together to develop clear and attainable job descriptions that detail the roles for both you and your partner in fulfilling these tasks.

How to Communicate Expectations

In the business world, the conflicts are often similar in origin to those in intimate relationships. While these conflicts between employer and employee may stem from many reasons, the main source is unfulfilled expectations. You may frequently hear examples of this in your daily work environment:

- *"I expected you to have known better; you are a longtime employee!"*
- *"No one else had a problem understanding what they were supposed to do!"*
- *"You were at the meeting where it was discussed, so I don't know why you didn't get the message!"*

If you fail to tell someone what your expectations are, then you cannot anticipate your expectations will be fulfilled to your standards, if at all.

Fixing this problem is not as easy as it seems. Just because we live in the information age with a myriad of communication choices doesn't mean that we've gotten any better at clearly talking or listening to each other; we all still assume far too much. In fact, communicating effectively has gotten even more difficult because we have too many opportunities to say the wrong thing, to be misinterpreted, or to forget to say what is important.

For example, as a consultant I will often begin a meeting, workshop, or retreat by having the participants (in small groups) ask each other a key question like, "What do you expect most out of today's meeting, from this initiative, or during your training session?" One person from the group then reports the group's findings, so that the others may see if the communication was delivered correctly and whether their expectations are aligned with what is planned. This is an attempt to address the biggest source of frustration and conflict in business relationships today: unfulfilled expectations, as mentioned above.

As another way to make this point, I will often go to the projector and turn the lens to defocus the image on the screen (a metaphor for the way people see and interpret things differently if they are not clearly spelled out). If roles and responsibilities are left fuzzy, then they are open for multiple interpretations, and this often sets the stage for conflict. So, be sure to get your relationship in focus!

The upside of these exercises is that you start out with the commitment to communicate clearly with each other, knowing fully what is expected of one another. To have an effective partnership, it is important that you match competencies and motivations with the tasks that need to be accomplished and the roles that must be fulfilled. In an orchestra, the flute player knows she won't be playing the kettledrum. In the same way that a place kicker knows he won't be playing quarterback in the next game, a good partnership needs strong "role clarity" so that both partners will work toward a specific set of common objectives by matching the tasks with the competencies of each partner. At the same time, good partners pitch in when needed and never adopt the "it's not my job" attitude!

In the past, especially in the case of our parents and their parents, household tasks were usually based on gender-specific job descriptions that clearly defined men's work and women's work, regardless of competencies. In times past, when work involved hard manual labor, it made sense that men would do the "heavy lifting"—but women played an equally important role in performing manual tasks within their abilities. Now, thanks to modern conveniences, laborsaving appliances, and the fact that most of us live in suburbs, not on farms, the basis for performing tasks has changed.

In business, it would be rare for someone to be given a task based solely on gender. Of course, if that did happen, there would be grounds for a gender discrimination lawsuit. Yet, couples do the exact same "illegal" thing all the time at home. Studies continually underscore the fact that most workingwomen believe the household work is to be shared. Men may agree with that in theory, but in practice, women are still doing the bulk of those household tasks. Men are simply not holding up their end of the bargain.

The core competencies of any live-in relationship include skills in life management, communication, negotiations and problem solving, sound mental and physical health, romance, and intimacy—yes, being romantic and intimate are skills that can be learned or enhanced.

In the contemporary cohabitating relationship, tasks ideally are driven by competency-based job descriptions. Each task is to be performed by the person who is the most competent, skilled, and motivated to perform them, regardless of gender. The man may cook and the woman may handle the finances. The man may garden and the woman may do the plumbing. The woman may do the travel planning and the man may be in charge of the social activities. The key is to break the stereotypical molds and match the task with the person most qualified to do the job: doing so makes sense in business, so why not at home?

In addition, keep in mind that you are modeling key values and showing others a certain philosophy of life by the tasks you choose and how you perform them. What kind of role model do you want to be? What message do you send to others when they see you sitting on the couch watching TV while your partner is the only one ever cleaning the house (even though you both work full time)? Does this fit with your vision and relationship brand? Is this the happy life described in your vision statement for you and your partner?

Here's another reality check: How do you think your partner will feel after months of doing all the tasks she loathes and you refuse to share? Do you think she'll feel kindly toward you for not lifting a finger to help with the most unpleasant or mundane chores? Relationships are based on cause and effect—and what you get is a direct result of what you give (or don't give).

Think back in your work experience to a time when you've seen a colleague or team member not pulling his weight or doing her fair share. How did that make you react? You probably felt resentful and angry. Now think about your partner's feelings when she does more than her fair share of work while you wonder why "she's lost that lovin' feeling!" I promise you that conflicts will arise if you and your partner do not mutually determine equitable job descriptions.

Elements of Your Work Job Description

It helps to look at your own job description from your place of work (if you have one). What are some of the common elements described in it? First, it may typically reference larger responsibilities, such as overseeing marketing, sales, operations, training, etc. Then, it probably focuses on specific tasks, such as implementing a process-improvement system, providing training programs, managing the budget or a profit-and-loss statement for the department, or overseeing the development of online content for the company's website. In other words, it states your larger responsibilities in the organization and then the specific tasks to make that larger role successful.

It works the same way with your relationship responsibilities. First, you decide who is doing the larger tasks like maintaining the household, taking care of the pets, grocery shopping, financial planning, etc. Then, you can move into more specific tasks, figuring out who does what around the house as well as outside of it.

Sample Corporate Job Description for a Sales Account Manager
The account manager's individual responsibilities include, but are not limited to, the following:
1. Plan and prioritize personal sales activities and customer/prospect contact towards achieving agreed business aims, including costs and sales—especially managing personal time and productivity.
2. Plan and manage personal business portfolio/territory/business according to an agreed market development strategy.
3. Manage product/service mix, pricing, and margins according to agreed aims.
4. Maintain and develop existing and new customers through appropriate propositions, ethical sales methods, and relevant internal liaison to optimize quality of service, business growth, and customer satisfaction.
5. Use customer and prospect contact activities tools and systems, and update relevant information held in these systems.
6. Plan/carry out/support local marketing activities to agreed budgets and timescales, and integrate personal sales efforts with other organized marketing activities, e.g., product launches, promotions, advertising, exhibitions, and telemarketing.
7. Respond to and follow up on sales inquiries using appropriate methods.
8. Monitor and report on market and competitor activities and provide relevant reports and information.
9. Record, analyze, report and administer according to systems and requirements.
10. Communicate, liaise, and negotiate internally and externally using appropriate methods to facilitate the development of profitable business and sustainable relationships.
11. Attend and present at external customer meetings and internal meetings with other company functions necessary to perform tasks and aid business development.
12. Attend training to develop relevant knowledge, techniques, and skills.
13. Adhere to health and safety policy, and other requirements relating to care of equipment.
14. Other tasks as assigned!

Writing Your Job Description

To get started, think of your relationship as an organization that has you and your partner in the executive roles—maybe Chairman and President or CEO and COO or co-CEOs or co-Presidents or Partners. The title is not as important as the concept that you are equally sharing the tasks and the authority. Next, review the dimensions and objectives for your relationship, created earlier in the book, to provide structure to the development of your job descriptions. All your previous hard work will now start to pay off. These dimensions and objectives will serve as a basis for the various tasks and responsibilities that need to be taken care of in your household and to manage your live-in life together.

When you write your job descriptions, you can either do it separately or together. Choose the way that works best for you as a couple. You probably have a good idea as to how you work best after working on the vision and objectives or developing your brand.

Write your own overview of what role(s) you've agreed to take on and have your partner do the same. This will provide a strong start to tackling the more specific responsibilities in the next section.

We have now arrived at the concrete elements of this relationship model. In other words, we have moved beyond the conceptual issues that can be difficult to determine and are now into the concrete issues that affect couples on a daily basis. The Example Worksheet below is provided to help you and your partner develop an inventory of the tasks that need to be performed as part of your relationship job description. Please note that you will also use these tasks in the next chapters on performance feedback, compensation, and benefits planning.

This Example Worksheet shows a sampling of the routine tasks necessary to sustain a typical live-in relationship. Consider starting with a blank page and use this list to stimulate your thinking as you brainstorm a comprehensive list that reflects your actual circumstances. Next, consider adding several columns, as shown, and place a check in the appropriate column to indicate who you think should perform each task or how it should be handled. Then sit with your partner and compare your lists to see where you agree and where you will need to discuss, compromise, or negotiate differences.

Also, try to estimate the number of hours involved in performing each task you have listed on a monthly basis and the cost of paying someone to accomplish each of these tasks.

Job Description Category / Task:	A	B	C	D	E	F	G	H	I	J
EXAMPLE – Partner Job Description Monthly Planning Worksheet										
	His	Hers	Ours	Rotate	Negotiate	Outsource	Neither	Don't know	# of Hours	Est. $ Cost
HOUSEHOLD CHORES										
maintaining computer, printers								√	3	$20
cleaning the bathroom					√				4	$50
ERRANDS										
dry cleaning	√								1	$125
taking care of prescriptions						√				$35
FOOD										
buying groceries					√				2	$500
cooking				√					9	$100
FINANCES										
paying bills		√							2	n/a
banking				√					1	n/a
PETS										
veterinary care for pets						√			1	$10
washing the dog			√						1	n/a
FAMILY MANAGEMENT										
planning trips & vacations			√						1	n/a
maintaining family calendar								√	1	n/a

An Added Word on Outsourcing

Many organizations have systematically outsourced to external vendors all but those tasks that they feel are "mission-critical." It is okay to consider doing the same in your relationship. Use modern technology to make your life easier. The Internet and an explosion of entrepreneurs have resulted in a never-ending list of services that you can buy if you and your partner cannot agree on or choose not to perform them. You may pick from doggie day care to in-home chefs, from online banking to on-demand laundry services, from part-time nannies to personal trainers, from professional complainers who act as your consumer advocate to "honey do" handyman services.

Therefore, you and your partner need only to agree on what is mission-critical to the relationship. I assure you that the list is short, leaving what is not mission-critical to be seriously considered for outsourcing. Remind each other that these tasks are not cast in stone and will predictably change over time. You can always go back, revisit, and change them next month or next year.

Fun Exercise: To make sure you don't lose sight of your partner's valuable contribution and hard work, consider switching roles. As the saying goes, "Walk a mile in my shoes." Spend an hour, day, or week in the other person's job. Sleep on the other side of the bed. Switch cars for a month. Change your routine! It is always good to understand what goes on in your partner's daily life. And it's a good way to achieve greater intimacy through greater understanding!

Partner Job Description Planning Worksheet

The following list is a sampling of the routine tasks necessary to sustain a typical household. Use the list as a starting point in developing a comprehensive list that reflects your actual circumstances. Place a check in the appropriate column to indicate who you think should perform each task. Then sit with your partner and compare your lists to see where you agree and what differences you need to discuss, compromise, or negotiate.

Also, in anticipation of an activity in the chapter on compensation and benefits, try to estimate the number of hours involved in performing the task on a monthly basis and the cost of paying someone to accomplish each task.

Job Description Category / Task:	A His	B Hers	C Ours	D Rotate	E Negotiate	F Outsource	G Neither	H Don't know	I # of Hours	J Est. Cost
ERRANDS										
dry cleaning										
taking care of prescriptions										
CHILDREN										
changing diapers										
reading bedtime stories										
bathing children										
driving children to school										
feeding children										
driving children to after-school events										
scheduling with children										
ensuring children perform their chores										

Job Description Category / Task:	A His	B Hers	C Ours	D Rotate	E Negotiate	F Outsource	G Neither	H Don't know	I # of Hours	J Est. Cost
FOOD										
buying groceries										
cooking										
CHORES										
doing laundry										
ironing										
maintaining/repairing appliances										
spraying for insects										
maintaining fireplace/firewood										
FINANCES										
paying bills										
banking										
investing										
maintaining files of all legal papers, documents, etc.										

Job Description Category / Task:	A His	B Hers	C Ours	D Rotate	E Negotiate	F Outsource	G Neither	H Don't know	I # of Hours	J Est. Cost
PETS										
veterinary care										
washing dog										
cleaning up after dog										
feeding										
walking dog										
HOUSEHOLD MANAGEMENT										
planning trips and vacations										
maintaining family calendar										
sending cards and gifts										
MISCELLANEOUS										

Job Description Category / Task:	A His	B Hers	C Ours	D Rotate	E Negotiate	F Outsource	G Neither	H Don't know	I # of Hours	J Est. Cost

Chapter Highlights:

- Recognizing the benefits of sharing household tasks with your partner, particularly if you both work outside the home
- Creating job descriptions and a detailed task list for both partners
- Preventing, reducing, or eliminating conflicts over household chores
- Learning the importance of shared household responsibilities to maintain the intimacy and kindness of your live-in relationship

Strategy #7
Relationship Feedback

*"Don't lower your expectations to meet your performance.
Raise your level of performance to meet your expectations.
Expect the best of yourself, and then do what is necessary
to make it a reality."*
—Ralph Marston, motivator and teacher.

Chapter Objectives:

1. Learn how to give and receive positive reinforcement.

2. Practice how to redirect behavior in a productive manner.

3. Set up a feedback process for you and your partner.

Successful Relationship Feedback

Once your job descriptions of roles and responsibilities in your relationship are clearly defined, it is time to discuss the best way to provide feedback about how well each of you is fulfilling your job description, as shown in the Job Description Planning Worksheet in the previous chapter.

If you are doing the things that you and your partner agreed on in the last chapter, there should be few problems. We all make mistakes and slack off on our tasks now and then. And when we do, the feedback we often get is highly negative and sounds like this: "How many times do I have to ask you to pick your socks up off the floor?" or "You are no better at keeping your word than my last roommate."

To avoid this kind of unproductive and damaging feedback, it is important to establish a productive process that does not have to be something you dread. This way when you have your relationship meetings and retreats as described later in this book, you'll have fewer negative things to discuss and a lot more positive accomplishments to celebrate.

For lack of a better word, "behavior" is used to describe how each of you is fulfilling your job description. Call it what you like; just be sure to not avoid talking about doing what you said you would do... it's about honesty and integrity in your job performance.

Now, let's look at how to provide positive feedback when your partner meets or exceeds expectations and how to successfully redirect behavior that falls short of expectations without diminishing your partner's self-concept. In most long-term relationships, partners remember to compliment each other every now and then. A guy will tell his gal she looks pretty, that he likes her hairstyle, or that she cooked a nice meal. A gal will tell her guy he did a good job on setting up all the home office equipment, or that he looks handsome today, or congratulate him on his promotion. These are very simple messages that all human beings need to feel appreciated or loved.

However, relationship feedback is more specific than a simple compliment. If you are going to take the time to provide feedback about how your partner has performed a task that is part of his or her job description, make sure that it really counts. Instead of simply saying, "Thanks for help in the kitchen," offer more descriptive and useful information. Try saying something like this: "The pantry looks great; it's so clean and organized... it's sure great to have your help with the work around the house!" The more descriptive and precise you are with the positive feedback, the more powerful the impact.

When giving feedback, be sure to use a common set of agreed-upon standards, perhaps determined in writing your objectives or identified in your job description. For example, if you followed the steps in the chapter on writing objectives, you might have discussed the dimension on Spirituality where you may have identified a core set of values and a code of conduct. This set of values and code of conduct can be the standard by which you evaluate each other's performance. The key is to have a unified set of standards that both partners use as the basis for feedback.

In a business setting, one key to effective feedback is when your supervisor's opinion is based on a common set of company values that serve as the basis for all behavior within the organization. Feedback is not given on a whim, based on the supervisor's mood, or impacted by bias or prejudice. It is consistent over time and is based on what behaviors are seen and heard, and whether or not these behaviors model company values.

At home, instead of just saying to your roommate, "Thanks for being a great partner," a good praising message would be, "I really appreciate how much patience you have when my kids come to visit since you have been so used to peace and quiet on the weekends."

In addition, it is important to note that a good praising message is typically a monologue, not a discussion. In telling your partner why you think a certain behavior is positive and productive, the most to expect is for your partner to give a simple "Thank you" or "You're welcome." You and your partner need to work on accepting each other's praising messages without debate and without discounting the significance of what is being acknowledged.

We all need to learn to do a better job of accepting praise and positive feedback. All too often, positive feedback is seen as a set up for something bad. It's natural to become suspicious, and wonder what the person really wants or to get ready for "the other shoe to drop!" Surprisingly for some, it is easier to accept criticism than to let the praise soak in and to truly accept the feedback as something we earned and deserve. If freely accepting positive feedback for yourself is difficult, it may mean that you don't give it freely either. Remember the best work you can do for the relationship is the work that you do on yourself... so get to work on overcoming barriers to being more open with your praise and recognition of your partner, if this is an issue.

Praising

When I conduct feedback training in businesses, I often ask a worthy and respected employee in the workshop to come up to the front of the room and then ask the other employees to give genuine comments on their actual experiences with their colleague, in the form of a very brief praising message. "Nicole, I really appreciate that every time I contact you about production schedules, you get right back to me. It shows that you are responsive and in support of our company value of teamwork. Thanks!" There is no further discussion—no ifs, ands or buts. It is just that simple.

Changing the Context

The most important part of giving praising messages, especially if it is uncharacteristic of your typical behavior, is to provide a context for your new behavior so your partner will not be suspicious. Tell your partner that you are going to be acting differently from now on.

Let's say, for example, that you hear a message about the importance of keeping romance alive in a relationship at your place of worship. Feeling a bit guilty, you take the message to heart and decide to stop on your way home from work and buy flowers for your partner since you have not done this in quite a while.

Without a proper context for your new behavior, when you proudly present the flowers to her, the first thing she might say is, "OK, what did you do wrong?" Instead, if you had told her beforehand that you were impacted by the message and were going to actively work to rekindle the romance, she would have a different context for your new behavior and not have been suspicious—instead, she is more likely to be delighted with the flowers. She simply needed a new context for your unexpected behavior, a simple explanation about why you are going to be acting differently!

Another thing to consider is that praising messages do not have to be face-to-face. You can give praising messages in an email, text message, voice mail, or hide a card in her suitcase before she leaves on a business trip. Giving a praising message doesn't have to be time-consuming. Use technology as another means to keep the romance alive.

Redirecting

As you can imagine, trying to redirect your partner's behavior can be more challenging and complex. Be sure to give your feedback when your partner has done something that does not meet the expectations of his or her job description, or is outside your shared religious beliefs, or does not fit with the core values that you both may have established when setting relationship objectives in the earlier chapter. Unlike praising, a redirecting message is meant to be a two-way discussion or dialogue. You will deliver your message, but then your partner needs to respond so you both can work on developing a mutually acceptable solution. However, before jumping to conclusions and prematurely setting the stage for a redirecting discussion, there are some questions you might consider before even talking with your partner:

1. Does your partner know the behavior does not meet your expectations?

_____

2. Does your partner know what you want or value instead?

_____

3. Are there obstacles beyond his or her control?

_____

4. Does your partner know how to do what you want?

_____

5. Could your partner do it if he or she wanted to?

_____

   If you consider all these questions and still end up with the realization that you need to talk with your partner about his or her behavior, here are some recommended steps to follow!

Delivering the Redirecting Message

   1. *Setting the stage*—Ask your partner for a few minutes to talk about something that has been bothering you. If possible, deliver your message as soon as you can after the undesired behavior has occurred. Be sure not to ambush your partner; set up a meeting time that works for you both, just as you would do at work.

   2. *Sharing your observations*—Remember to describe the specific behavior and how it does not seem to be in keeping with what you both value. Example: "Three times this weekend I heard you yell at Billy because he wouldn't turn down the television!"

_____

_____

3. *Explaining your expectations*—Be specific and tell your partner the specific behavior you want instead. "I'd like to see you be more patient with him when he doesn't cooperate right away and to find a way to..."

_____

_____

_____

4. *Listen to your partner's response*—When it comes time for your partner to respond, it is likely that the response will be defensive, even if you try not to sound accusatory. The odds are high that your partner will feel guilty, frustrated, or inept. It is natural to try to justify a behavior and explain it away. Listen patiently and let your partner have his or her say. After all, you might learn something that you did not know that explains the behavior. Ask clarifying questions, "Is there something that gets in the way of being patient with him?"

_____

_____

_____

_____

_____

5. *Develop a solution*—With your partner's input, negotiate a realistic and mutually agreed-upon solution to the behavior that you are trying to redirect. Be patient and work together to generate possible solutions. People are more likely to comply with solutions they help create. If they cannot or will not offer solutions, make your own suggestions about how the behavior might be redirected. "Should we trade off on tasks with him for a few weeks?" "Is there something I can do for you to make this go more smoothly?" Remember, the key is to focus not on who is right, but instead on what is right, and in this example, what is right for your son!

6. *Follow-up*—All redirecting discussions usually include follow-up to ensure that the behavior has changed or is improving. Put a date on your calendar and plan to talk with your partner in a day, week, or a month to review progress. If there has been improvement, reinforce the new behavior with positive feedback. But do not expect perfection! If the behavior does not change, schedule another session. Old habits die hard, and it may take several sessions before the undesirable behavior is successfully redirected.

Giving Relationship Feedback

Now that you understand how to give both praising and redirecting messages about a single behavior, we can move on to the all-important comprehensive feedback process. Typically, in the business environment, the formal performance feedback process is disliked and rarely done effectively. Most research shows that neither the person giving nor the person getting the feedback likes the process. All too often, performance feedback at work fails to provide meaningful information that can be turned into actions or is so vague that it offers little differentiation between poor and excellent performance.

Regardless of these commonly held beliefs, if done correctly, it can be very satisfying and rewarding to hear concrete examples and specific ratings of how well you are performing your job. If a company's employees are performing well, you can bet that business is likely to be successful, too. The opposite is also true: business failure is often due, in part, to employees who are not performing their jobs well.

Ideally, an employee's annual performance feedback is based on his or her job description. If an employee is fired for failing to perform a job he or she was never asked to do, it may result in a complaint or even a lawsuit. Similarly, it is not fair to criticize your partner for not performing a task or meeting a standard that person never agreed to fulfill.

Therefore, setting up clear expectations for how each of you will perform your jobs and responsibilities is a key element to a successful relationship. Talk about your job descriptions and make sure you each understand to what standard these tasks are to be completed.

For instance, if you've taken on cleaning the bathrooms once a week, discuss what your idea of a clean bathroom is. If your partner is a perfectionist or clean freak with a contamination phobia, make sure you can agree on a standard of cleanliness. Additionally, make sure you can live with how your partner will perform his or her tasks. The more specific you can be about expectations, the less likely it is that you'll fight over various interpretations of performance.

If you are responsible for grocery shopping, make sure you know what specific items your family members need to have for their daily lives or how to know when it is time to purchase groceries. Or if you are in charge of helping the kids with homework, make sure you and your partner are clear as to how much help and time you plan to offer. Once the standards are set, you can easily fold them into a regular relationship feedback process.

Creating a Relationship Feedback Form

In your place of employment, your organization may use some type of standardized form that your supervisor asks you to fill out on yourself before your regular feedback meeting. This is a good idea for you and your partner as well. It gives you an idea as to the areas in which you think you fall behind or excel before you see your partner's opinions. When you compare forms, you may be surprised to learn that your partner thinks you are doing a good job in areas that you didn't feel were your best efforts. Or you may be perfectly aligned.

The easiest way to begin the feedback process is to use the job descriptions that you (hopefully) developed previously as a basis for the feedback you give your partner, as shown below. In Part 1 of the example form, consider each task on the list that is part of your or your partner's job description. Then think back over an agreed-upon period of time, preferably 90 to 180 days, and then select the number that most accurately reflects how well you feel that you or your partner has completed this task. In Part 2, be sure to add comments to further clarify any task where you might have given a "Does not meet expectations" or "Exceeds expectations!" For example, take the grocery shopping duty. A score of 3 would mean you are never in want for anything when you go into the kitchen, and a score of 1 could mean you are always out of bread and toilet paper.

In our household, we are often out of milk and end up running out to the store to get it just for our coffee in the morning. Since my partner has agreed to buy groceries as part of her job description, she gets lower marks for this responsibility! While we joke about this and approach these types of discussions in a caring, lighthearted, and positive manner, we both still know that avoiding dealing with disappointments in the little things can lead to bigger issues going unresolved as well.

Remember that the focus of this activity is to provide feedback to your partner. Just as in business, it is meant to be a tool to strengthen the relationship, clarify expectations, and ensure that the day-to-day tasks of being in a relationship do not get in the way of an ever-deepening friendship built on trust, mutual respect, intimacy, and forgiveness.

It may be uncomfortable the first time you give and receive feedback, but look at it as taking the more proactive route by having a systematic way to give feedback on agreed-to tasks. You will bypass the unproductive comments and criticisms that come from weeks (or maybe years) of frustration and anger stemming from unfulfilled expectations or poor performance. Approaching the feedback process with a caring attitude and a spirit of friendly cooperation will go a long way toward establishing regular feedback as one of the most powerful and positive events that you and your partner can build into the foundation of your relationship.

Sample Relationship Feedback – Part 1			
Performance Checklist	Does not meet expectations	Meets expectations	Exceeds expectations
1. buying groceries	√		
2. paying bills			√
3. caring for pets		√	
4. feeding children			√
5. maintaining computer, printers		√	
6. changing diapers			√
7. reading bedtime stories			√
8. cleaning bathroom	√		
9. dry cleaning			√
10. vacuuming			√
11. cooking		√	
12. yard work			
13. car maintenance	√		
14. house maintenance	√		
15. banking			√
16. investing		√	
17. maintaining family calendar			√
18. driving children to school			√
19. driving children to after-school events			√
20. taking care of prescriptions			√
21. changing bedding			√
22. laundry			√
23. sending cards and gifts			√
24. cleaning garage		√	
25. setting up date night		√	
26. scheduling time with children			√
27. cleaning outside porches	√		
28. washing dog		√	
29. bathing children			√
30. taking garbage out		√	
31. maintaining the pool		√	

Relationship Feedback—Part 2

Examples of additional comments:

Exceeding expectations:

"You are the best partner I've ever seen. You are more patient, accepting and loving than I could ever be!"

Meets expectations:

"Thanks for finding time to cook in the middle of everything else you are juggling!"

Does not meet expectations:

"We are often out of milk and dog food which makes it difficult on me when trying to make breakfast, and I feel guilty when I only have table scraps to feed the dog!"

Formalize the Process

Establish a mutually convenient time, duration, and frequency for your feedback sessions—at least one or two hours every 90 to 180 days. Be sure to plan ahead and mark a date on your calendar so you don't forget to prepare yourself and so forth. The frequency of these meetings will be based on how important feedback is to your relationship. If you are living with children and you both work hectic schedules, it might be more important for you to meet more frequently, even if for only a few minutes at a time. Meeting once every few months may be enough if you are in a long-term, live-in relationship and are living a stable and leisurely lifestyle. If you are somewhere in between, you may want to meet twice per year. It's up to you. Choose the frequency that is best for you and your partner's needs. Complete the forms on each other in advance, and then sit down and go through each item together. See the chapter on Meetings and Retreats for more information on conducting these types of meetings. Remember that the formal feedback process is supplemented with praising and redirecting discussions that occur on a regular basis, as necessary or appropriate. While this ongoing feedback is not a replacement for the formalized process, it is also best not to wait long periods to provide feedback.

If done correctly, there will be no surprises when you have your formal face-to-face meeting. Because you have agreed to do certain tasks to a specific standard, it is unlikely that you will be shocked to get a low score on something you haven't been accomplishing well. Similarly, you will likely be delighted to hear positive feedback and receive high scores in the areas of your job description where you feel most competent.

Finally, keep in mind that it is important to remain flexible with the various tasks on each job description. Circumstances change, motivation will vary, competencies may increase or someone may tire of doing a particularly mundane, difficult, or unpleasant task. Remember that negotiation and compromise are critical to the long-term success of the relationship. Don't let conflict and tension about daily roles and responsibilities sap the romance and commitment from your partnership.

Chapter Highlights:

- Learning how to give positive, praising reinforcement
- Learning how to redirect behavior in a productive manner
- Setting up a process for you and your partner to give regular feedback

Strategy #8

Compensation and Benefits

*"You know you are on the road to success if you would do your job,
and not be paid for it."*

—Oprah Winfrey, entertainer and entrepreneur

Chapter Objectives:

1. Discover what motivates us to be in the relationship so that we can ensure our motivation will continue.
2. Measure the monetary value you bring to your relationship and quality of life.
3. Create a "benefits package" for your relationship.
4. Sign a contract that spells out all the important things you want and need from your relationship.

Getting Paid

I know what you are likely asking yourself right now: "Compensation? I get money for being in a relationship?" Well, you don't get cash-based compensation, but if you have a healthy and intimate relationship, you do get something that money cannot buy—an "emotional paycheck." This chapter will explore the compensation and benefits of being in a successful, live-in relationship.

Motivators

The first thing we need to do is realize the motivation behind the things we choose to do as well as the relationships we choose to be in. While the motive may not be evident at the time, we always have reasons for our actions—behavior is the physical manifestation of an underlying motive. If you grew up in a positive, loving home where Dad was the breadwinner, Mom was the homemaker, and it seemed to work well for them, the odds are that you will be motivated to recreate that model in your own relationship despite your own claims to the contrary.

If, on the other hand, your parents were both troubled, dysfunctional alcoholics, you will understandably be motivated to build a relationship as different as possible from that of your own parents. Understanding the motives for your relationship can be illuminating and unsettling at the same time. For the purpose of this chapter, let's agree that there is a payoff for your relationship even if you don't know what it is now. But you will need to understand what the motivations are to ensure that you keep getting "paid!"

In business, how to motivate yourself and others is often the subject of debate. While there is no simple or clear formula for what will increase motivation in others, it is accurate to say that different employees are motivated by different things.

First, many employers think they know what motivates their employees and will often cite more money, greater job security, or opportunities for promotion. All of these things cost the company money. Interestingly enough, studies show that employees often cite a very different list of motivations for working, such as being appreciated for the quantity or quality of work performed, a feeling of "being in on things," help with personal problems, or the loyalty of their supervisor. All of these elements have an emotional base and do not cost money.

I give this information to my clients because what truly motivates an employee to give his or her *all* at work is not always perceived correctly by the employer. The same thing applies to our partners. While you may think you know what motivates your partner, the truth is that unless you explore your motivation for living together and discuss it with your partner, it is unlikely that you know what your partner (or you, for that matter) needs in his or her "emotional paycheck" to feel rewarded.

So take a few minutes to think about what motivates you to be with your partner, what motivates you to stay in the relationship, and what you think will keep you motivated in the future? Ask your partner to do the same and then tell each other what you have (re)discovered. Be forewarned: you may be surprised or even shocked to hear what's really going on in your partner's mind.

Determining Your "Emotional Paycheck"

In business, you get paid for the work that you perform based on the value you contribute to your company's bottom line. It is similar living together since you add value to the relationship based on the tasks you perform in your job description. Just for fun, you may want to figure out the value of what you do for the relationship that you don't actually get paid to do. Consider adding up the costs of outsourcing the tasks on your job description. Go back to your Job Description Planning and be sure to complete column "I," where you estimate the number of hours you spend performing that task on a monthly basis. Then complete column "J," where you estimate what it would cost to pay someone to perform that task if you had to buy the service on the open market.

Estimating the number of hours will likely be easier than estimating the cost to buy that service, but accuracy is not the point. Instead, the point is to see your relationship in a different light and to understand that you contribute to and derive value from your relationship. In a live-in relationship, each partner is valued for the contribution he or she makes to the relationship, whether bringing home a paycheck or staying at home to jump-start your home-based business.

In reality, these contributions may not have the same monetary value, but it is critical that they be seen as having equal emotional value. This is the worth of your contribution to and compensation for the relationship, something you can feel empowered by and proud of. There is no need to argue about who contributes more… partners are different, but both contribute equally and are compensated equally.

Developing Your "Benefits Package"

On the other side of relationship compensation are the benefits you get from living together. In business, the benefits package encompasses the all-important items that customarily come with the job, such as health and dental insurance, pensions, retirement funds and 401Ks, holiday parties, travel and entertainment expense accounts, flexible hours, telecommuting, maternity leave, paid time off, and so on. In addition to these ready-made benefits, you also (hopefully) receive the benefit of increased self-worth, camaraderie with colleagues you respect, increased job knowledge, learning new skills, and feeling useful and valued.

The same feelings apply to a healthy and intimate live-in relationship. Your benefits might be as simple as being loved and understood or having a satisfying sex life or daily companionship. Other benefits of being together can be such varied things as having a gourmet dinner companion or being with someone who shares your interest in taking adventurous trips. Perhaps you benefit by competing in who can be most romantic, or in sharing your faith journey, or in achieving financial serenity, and more.

Along with your emotional paycheck discussed earlier, you might consider coming up with a statement that describes your relationship "benefits package."

For example, your statement could simply be:

"As a result of living with you, I'll have a good role model for my kids, a wonderful life of travel and adventure, no worries about money, and fun-filled days and nights."

Another example could be,

"The reason I am accepting this 'job' offer to be your partner is to feel love and support every day as we live together, with romance, fulfilling sexual relations, and companionship as a part of our daily existence."

Because the preferred benefits package can be unique for each individual in the partnership, it is hard to develop a general list of benefits that fits everyone. However, as you would when you negotiate with a potential new employer after they have extended you a job offer, here are some questions to consider to help identify what benefits are important to you and to serve as the basis for developing your relationship benefits package:

1. How do you want to be appreciated for the contribution of the "emotional paycheck" to the relationship?

---

2. What is the best method for your partner to show you that he/she loves you?

---

3. How do you prefer to celebrate special events, e.g., birthdays?

---

4. How do you like to be shown physical affection (in public)?

---

5. When you have done something that benefits your relationship in an extraordinary way, how would you like it to be acknowledged?

_____

_____

6. When you have had a particularly pressured and stressful day, how would you like your partner to show her or his empathy and support?

_____

_____

Once you have answered these and any other questions that you feel are pertinent to determining what you want in your benefits package, you can write a statement describing the benefits of your relationship, as it exists today. It is okay if this evolves over time.

Your Relationship Benefits Statement

It takes the vision of your relationship to a more individual, "what's in it for me" level, which of course is why you are there in the first place. It's your motivation for being living together.

_____

_____

_____

The Cohabitation Contract

Essentially, a live-in relationship is an unwritten contract between you and your partner. The only unfortunate part is that all too often, because it is unwritten, it is vague, open to interpretation, selectively forgotten or rationalized away. Agreeing on a Cohabitation Contract can be useful in making sure you both remember why it is you got into this relationship in the first place.

Many companies have employment contracts with their employees, particularly for senior management, that state the terms of the relationship and the rights each entity carries into the relationship. The major issues within an employee contract are compensation, tasks and responsibilities, performance evaluation, and a few other necessary legalities. We've already talked about many of these issues, but now you may want to commit to them formally, in contract form. The Cohabitation Contract is the foundation to ensure that your relationship is successful, productive, and sustainable for as long as it makes sense.

A contract can incorporate the meaningful things that have been said to each other along the way. It could contain elements of your vision for the relationship and how you will maintain and nurture it. It could include a list of needs and wants (like your emotional paycheck and compensation package that you just detailed) and how you will satisfy each other's expectations for the relationship.

As an example, what follows is a modified sample relationship contract written by students at a community college and is now in the public domain. While it may have elements that are not relevant to your relationship, such as blended families and stepchildren, you may still find it a useful tool as a basis for developing your own relationship contract, or at least it may provide the basis for more intimate conservations with your partner.

COHABITATION CONTRACT

My name:

My partner's name:

1. General statement about why we are moving in with each other and our general values and philosophy of living together:

    *   We need and want a healthy relationship and believe that we will be able to resolve difficulties as long as we have the motivation to do so. Motivation is essential for sustaining a relationship.

    *   We love and value each other. We each have knowledge of failed relationships. A sound and healthy relationship is still very appealing to each of us in spite of this. We feel that we would benefit from the nurturing that we need and that this relationship would provide.

2. A description of specific behavior we plan and expect from each other in each of the following areas:

    Money

    *   Each of us is moving in together free from debt. We plan to have a joint bank account.

    *   We will save the first 10% of our gross earnings for a mutually agreed-upon annual vacation planned together in advance, and to save another 5% of gross earnings for emergencies, and, if not needed, for a mutually planned expenditure.

    *   Rent, utilities, food, transportation, insurance payments and contributions will come from the joint bank account.

- Any loans or donations to friends or relatives will be mutually agreed upon in advance before being offered to the person in need.

Sex

- We agree that monogamous intimate relations between partners is essential for trust.
- We will try to understand and respect the sexual desires of each other.
- We agree upon frequent sex for mutual enjoyment and fulfillment, and agree not to use it as a power play in the relationship.

Work

- We agree that, beyond financial necessity, careers provide healthy ego and social satisfaction.
- Present careers are to be maintained and any future career changes are to be mutually decided and supported.

Children

- We agree that resident and non-resident children need to be accommodated. We have agreed to accept each other's children.
- Duties and responsibilities for each blended family member are to be mutually planned and communicated to the children.
- We have also agreed to allow children, regardless of age, to spend time alone with the natural parent when needed. We will support the extra nurturing given by the natural parent.

Relatives

- We have agreed to accept and respect our relatives despite their possible criticism of our living arrangement.
- We will alternate with each other's families in order to keep up family traditions of participation in holiday dinners.

- Birthday parties, weddings, funerals, and other special occasions will be attended when possible as a couple.

Residences

- We plan to agree to a principal residence in the community we mutually select.
- If one of us should decide upon a career change, we will collaborate on a choice of residence.

Friends

- We agree to accept each other's friends, and have already accepted our friends of the past. Time and activities will be mutually planned and agreed upon.
- We'll each respect best friends of the other and allow for time alone with them when desired.

Recreation

- We have agreed to mutually plan and share vacations and other times of recreation.
- If one partner should wish to plan recreation with children alone, it will also be mutually agreed upon.

Religion

- One of us is Protestant and the other Catholic. We believe in the basic tenets of our respective religions, and are tolerant and respectful of the beliefs of our partner.
- We have agreed to the participation to some degree in our partner's religious tradition, and each expects reciprocation.

General Problem-Solving Techniques

- We have agreed to open discussion for at least ten minutes as problems surface to initiate steps for resolution. Then, we will part for individual contemplation for at least one hour before returning to open discussion.

- If this cannot be sustained, the discussion will be postponed for twenty-four hours, and then restarted. If this fails, outside counseling should be initiated.

Duration of Contract

- We enter into this cohabitation arrangement without making a permanent, long-term commitment. While we hope a successful, sustainable relationship will evolve as a result of cohabitating, we also realize that we will be living together on a trial basis, only. Therefore, we agree to re-evaluate and either extend or renegotiate this entire contract _____ from today.

Signed:

Partner 1 _____ Date: _____

Partner 2 _____ Date: _____

Do You Feel the Love?

By now, you have a good sense of what you and your partner need most out of your relationship to feel valued and "well-paid." You may even have a formal contract to prove it! You may also want to compare your results with your vision and objectives to ensure they are all aligned. At the end of it all, make sure these different elements of your emotional pay make you feel well compensated and abundantly rewarded. Remember, this chapter is simply about identifying your motives for being in the relationship. We all have them, and the more you know about yours, the better partner you can be.

In the next chapter, we will discuss meetings and retreats as an effective means to manage the day-to-day tasks of being in the relationship or as a special, dedicated period during which you will be reviewing your vision and objectives to evaluate how well your entire relationship enterprise is working. Now it's time to schedule a meeting or set the date for that all-important retreat to revisit all your hard work.

Chapter Highlights:

- Understanding what motivates you and your partner to be in the relationship
- Detailing your monetary contribution to the relationship and knowing the amount of your emotional paycheck
- Writing down the emotional benefits of being with each other
- Exploring options for writing a relationship contract as the basis for a long-term commitment

Strategy #9
Meetings and Retreats

"Life is what happens while you're busy making other plans."
—John Lennon, singer, musician, artist, and writer

Chapter Objectives:

1. Introduce how to hold regular meetings to conduct the business of your relationship.

2. Understand the guidelines to running effective relationship meetings on a regular basis.

3. Plan an annual retreat to fully reevaluate and refuel your relationship.

Let's Do Lunch

The common complaint from many employees in all types of organizations is, "Meetings, meetings, and more meetings! Sometimes it seems that rather than getting any real work done, all we do is attend meetings!" Interestingly enough, couples often complain of the opposite: that the partners are both so busy that they never find time to meet and really talk about what is going on in their lives and their relationship.

While we might all agree that there is always a need to improve communication through meetings, companies often actually damage communication by holding an endless series of unproductive meetings. It is no wonder that the idea of holding regular meetings with your partner might not sound like the most exciting way to spend time together.

However, in the best of circumstances, properly run meetings can be a highly effective method to keep the flow of communication strong, to move projects and ideas forward, and to conduct business. When a business meeting is managed the right way, it can create a better, more effective working environment.

The same can be said about relationship meetings. Holding regular meetings to conduct the business of your relationship is one of the most effective strategies to enhance satisfaction and prevent more serious problems in the future. While this proposition may make sense, our busy lives don't always allow for uninterrupted discussions about the everyday issues that must be managed between partners. Life does happen anyway, so you have a choice either to be purposeful in your interactions and communication patterns with your partner or to risk negative consequences.

Spontaneous and Purposeful Meetings

The fact is that you are most likely already having spontaneous meetings, like the typical passing discussions about your work schedule or activities at home during breakfast, on your cell phone on the way home from work, in a series of text messages, or in a string of emails. If you are having these discussions already, and if they are effective, don't abandon this approach. These informal, spontaneous discussions often get the job done. The bottom line is that you are taking the time amid all the distractions of life to talk about what is going on in your life.

While I encourage these spontaneous meetings whenever there's a need, I also would like you to consider the importance of setting up a purposeful, structured, face-to-face relationship meeting on a regular basis. For many couples, having a consistent meeting on the first and third Tuesday of the month (or whatever day suits you) brings a sense of comfort because each partner knows that there is a dedicated time set aside to talk about the minor and major issues of the relationship. These planned meetings are a time to talk about the business of the relationship, roles and responsibilities, upcoming events and general problems (excluding redirecting of behavior sessions about your partner's job performance).

In addition, the purposeful couple's meetings described here are different than the discussions that you may already have at the dinner table. However, couples still need to dedicate meeting time to discuss the business of their relationship.

Guidelines for a Purposeful Couple's Meeting

Certain techniques for running an effective meeting can be applied to your formal couple meetings, as follows:

1. Be sure to write an agenda.

2. Estimate the amount of time you will need to talk about any given topic on the agenda.

3. Describe the outcome you need when covering each agenda item.

4. Be sure to write down the decisions made and actions to be taken.

5. Keep the discussion focused on agenda items only—do not pad the meeting with other items unless there is mutual agreement.

6. Don't ambush—discussing problematic behavior is best set aside for a single-item meeting.

7. Be sure to start and end the meeting on time.

One last guideline: no multi-tasking allowed. Multitasking typically means doing several things at the same time, poorly. Consider how you would feel if, in the middle of lovemaking, your partner pulled out the checkbook and starting reconciling the bank statement? It just isn't a good idea. The same thing goes for when you and your partner are attending the couple's meeting. You need uninterrupted time to discuss the business of your relationship. The meeting is sacred, the time protected, the TV and phones off.

In addition, if it is not already part of your job description, consider rotating the "facilitator" role so each of you takes responsibility for making these meetings valuable. See below for a sample agenda.

Sample Agenda: Monthly Couple Information Meeting

Jenny's Topics

1. Weekend activities—5-7 minutes—need to agree which events to support and how to integrate them into the overall schedule.

2. Bill payment—2 minutes—make the final decision to switch to online bill payment.

3. Vacation plans—10 minutes—present the latest information about the beach vs. mountain trip, costs, accommodations, dates, etc.

4. Business trip—5 minutes—discuss conflicts with niece's upcoming recital.

5. Gift-buying—2 minutes—decide what to buy for my brother's birthday.

Steve's Topics

1. Weekend chores—3 minutes—determine the priority of the "honey do" list.

2. Financial planning—2 minutes—set the meeting with the banker.

3. Car maintenance—5 minutes—decide what to do while the SUV is in the shop.

4. Upcoming projects—10 minutes—present the estimated budget for the added deck and patio furniture.

5. Business trip—5 minutes—discuss conflicts with weekend softball game.

Agenda: Monthly Couple Meeting	
Partner's Topics	Time Needed
❏	
❏	
❏	
❏	
❏	
❏	
❏	
❏	
❏	
❏	
❏	

To keep meetings useful, be sure to occasionally take a few minutes at the end to evaluate the effectiveness of the meetings. Are they too far apart, not long enough, the wrong time of day, irrelevant, meaningful, productive? Don't be afraid to make adjustments to ensure the meetings remain of value to you both.

You can add intimate touches to these meetings, too. Start or end each meeting with a prayer or one positive life experience each of you has had since the last meeting. While having a redirecting discussion about a partner's job performance is off-limits, I encourage you to spontaneously give a praising message: "You know, we get so much done at these meetings because you are so good at keeping us focused on the important issues. Thanks for running these meetings." Or, "Thanks for doing all that research on vacations. It really helps us to narrow the choices to a few places. This will make our decision so much easier." See, it's easy—and it gives your partner something to feel good about. The key is to make the meetings something you look forward to each time.

Adding Structure, Reducing Complexity

When you are discussing many different types of issues in a single meeting, it can add complexity that becomes disruptive. For instance, if you are discussing your job frustration and doing vacation planning in the same meeting, it can be hard to tackle such emotionally diverse issues in the same discussion.

Instead, consider planning the agenda in a sequence that starts with the fun, simple, and easy issues before tackling those more challenging aspects of your relationship. Or do just the opposite, and save the fun stuff for last, to end on a positive note. Consider taking a break between the easy and challenging topics, or even plan on having two different meetings. In addition, consider the different types of meetings, and be sure to select the meeting format most appropriate for the items on the agenda. Do you need to make decisions, solve problems, share information, or do planning?

For instance, an informational meeting (again, see the sample agenda) could simply provide basic information as to what is going on in your life. A decision-making meeting could be to finalize a car purchase or to start planning a job change. A problem-solving meeting may seek to address your partner's health problems. Planning meetings can be a fun time to plan vacations or brainstorm home improvement ideas.

You can also combine some of the meetings: for example, a mixture of information and making plans, or a mixture of finalizing the decision of which dental specialist to use and coming up with other solutions to your work-related problems. Any combination can work, assuming one agenda item isn't so contentious that it overrides the other items on the agenda.

Retreat and Recharge!

If meetings are about the day-to-day business of living together (like the objectives in each dimension of your relationship or the tasks on your job description), a retreat is a once- or twice-a-year getaway to fully reevaluate and refuel your relationship. It is truly a retreat from your daily life and is meant to be both positive and productive.

When businesspeople go away on a retreat, they get out of the office or they close the office for the day so there are no distractions. Companies often use this time to look at their long-range vision, to evaluate progress in meeting objectives, and to establish new targets for the business. At some retreats, companies ask their employees to come up with creative new ideas that could take the company in a different direction. Whatever the content of a business retreat, it usually focuses on the higher-level company issues rather than the daily business that a staff meeting would cover.

Partner retreats do not happen at the kitchen table or over email. They do not happen in the car on the way home from work together. A retreat is that special time to go away and just be with one another. Maybe you can find a special in the newspaper for a local hotel and spa, or maybe you'd prefer to camp out in the wilderness. If you have an annual vacation, there might be times during that break to also have your retreat. All you need is a copy of your vision statement and brand logo, objectives, job descriptions, performance feedback, and each other.

You need to have a few dedicated large blocks of time to cover a prepared agenda: revisiting and reevaluating the vision and objectives, getting an update on the financial picture, and other long-term issues appropriate to your living together. No matter where you go, make sure you have these blocks of time where no one will bother you, except perhaps for a waiter delivering room service.

At some time during this retreat, remember to schedule a formal performance feedback meeting, as mentioned earlier, and a discussion about your compensation and benefits, as well. Remember, during the mutual performance feedback discussion, there should be no surprises because, ideally, you both have been praising and redirecting throughout the year. The performance discussion is simply a summary of all the feedback you've given and received during those discussions over the past few months. In addition, this is the time to verify with your partner that you are still investing in the relationship by fulfilling the roles on your job description and that you are feeling sufficiently gratified by what you are receiving in return.

If you must stay at home to have your retreat, keep one important factor in mind:

NO INTERRUPTIONS - turn off the televisions, phones, Blackberrys, pagers, etc. and all the other distractions of your normal daily life.

Try to create a different atmosphere in your home that does not include doing dishes or returning e-mail. Just as with the purposeful relationship meetings, be sure to evaluate the retreat to ensure it was helpful and a worthwhile investment in your relationship. Balance the "fun" and "work" sides of this valuable time away. If you need to modify things for next year's retreat, do so. Practice makes perfect!

I also encourage you to play and have fun between the big blocks of dedicated retreat time, especially if you engage in team-building efforts like snorkeling, couples massage, golfing, lovemaking, and so on. Think about what elements of your own company retreats you really liked and incorporate them, as appropriate.

Most of all, be sure to enjoy your time alone together and be romantic. Watch the sunset, take long walks, sit together in silence gazing at the ocean, and talk. I mean, really talk. The goal of your relationship (and this book) is for you to reach a level of intimacy with your partner that brings together the best of friendship and an ever-deepening love.

Chapter Highlights:

- Recognizing the value of incorporating regular meetings into your life, no matter how busy you are
- Learning to run an effective formal meeting with your partner
- Planning your next retreat with your partner to recharge your relationship

The "BUSINESS" MODEL

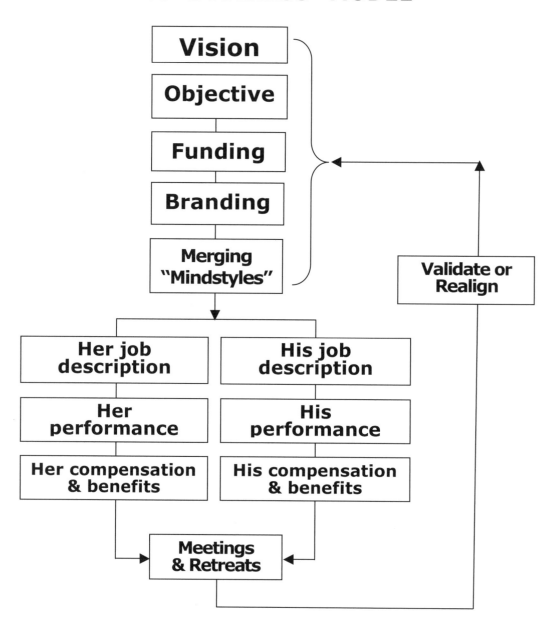

The Commencement

"Be who you are and say what you feel, because those who mind don't matter and those who matter don't mind."

—Dr. Seuss, author

The Beginning of the Rest of Your Relationship

You've made it through this book, but hopefully not untouched. Reading this book was not supposed to be just simply fun or easy... nothing worthwhile ever is. Feel proud of yourself for being open-minded enough to explore a different way to think about yourself and your relationship. The number one obstacle to self-development is self-deception. I think it would be hard to make it from cover-to-cover of this book and still be deceiving yourself.

By reading this book, you have chosen to consider a new approach to a live-in relationship. Like it or not, living together in advance of getting legally married (if that is your intent) does NOT increase your likelihood of success. In reality, those who cohabitate and then marry are MORE likely to divorce... but it does not have to happen to you. You might have recognized that you don't want to live a fantasy and pretend you are Romeo and Juliet (who both died in the play) living happily ever after. That's enough on what you don't want to do; let's discuss what you do want to do from here.

This book provides a clear, straightforward approach to building or enhancing a live-in relationship. Coming up with a vision and S.M.A.R.T. objectives for your relationship is not a simple task. Exploring attitudes about money, branding your relationship, or merging "mindstyles" is not easy either. Neither is writing a relationship job description, giving performance feedback, or determining what compensation and benefits you get from the relationship. Finally, meeting to discuss it all every year isn't for the weak-willed or faint of heart.

But I promise you that if you do these things and apply yourself to the strategies in this book, your relationship will flourish in ways that you never imagined. As you have seen, you can create a structure for your relationship in which love, authenticity, and a sense of friendship can thrive unencumbered by problems that typically undermine contemporary relationships founded on failed relationship models of the past.

I believe this is the first book you have read about using the business model as the foundation for a live-in relationship. This book has brought together the two separate worlds of intimate relationships and business. I hope it has made the case for taking a business approach to building your live-in relationship. While these separate worlds are indeed very different, they are comparable in that they require similarly high levels of purposeful effort to make them successful. This book is my contribution to the transformation of a live-in relationship so it might become healthier, happier, and permanent!

Romance Versus Intimacy

If you use the strategies outlined in this book, you and your partner will have a much more stable, mature relationship than before. You will reach the most satisfying closeness that a couple can achieve: intimacy, and a sense of warmth, closeness, and ease with your life and your partner that allows romance to flourish.

Intimacy is saying, "I know everything about you and I still love and care about you. I am committed to your growth and I support you, as I know you support me. We both make sacrifices for the other so that each of us can have the best relationship possible." When you can honestly say or feel this in your heart, you've reached the highest level of relationship intimacy. Of course, this is not to say that there won't be any challenges in your relationship from here on out, but you now have tools to help negotiate and resolve any issue that might arise!

Revisit the book's main model below, using business strategies to improve the bottom line of your relationship. It's a continually renewing model that starts and ends with your vision statement. If you had trouble in the beginning of this book writing and agreeing on a common vision, go back now and make sure you have some sense of what you want your relationship to focus on.

From the vision statement flows a logical set of measurable objectives. Then you are ready to explore attitudes about money, develop and market your relationship brand, create detailed job descriptions, provide constructive feedback, determine your emotional paycheck, and hold regular meetings and retreats. Whether you merge or acquire to form your relationship, these strategies from the business world will keep your relationship on the right track!

This is a cause-and-effect world where you get what you give. Think about it: a full-time job means working hundreds of hours a year. Now, most would agree that your live-in relationship is more important than your job! So, imagine what would happen if you pledged to invest 1/10th of the time you spend on the job working on your relationship. You'll be giving your partner 200 or more hours of relationship time. I don't mean sitting at home watching TV with your partner. Instead, I am asking that you consider how powerful, positive, and fulfilling your relationship could be if you both invested this many hours in building and sustaining a world-class relationship.

Free Will

You have a choice: You can either accept the poor odds of being in a successful live-in relationship, or you can build an intimate relationship that actually works in today's world. This, however, means you must be a historian and learn from the past; and you must be a pioneer and courageously go where no one has gone before, using a radically different approach. Open your eyes, look at yourself in the mirror, and become someone worth spending a lifetime with. A world-class relationship is within your grasp!

About the Author

John Curtis, Ph.D. is a researcher, organizational development consultant, business trainer and author. Prior to that, John was a full-time marriage and family counselor and was a clinical member of the American Association for Marriage and Family Therapy. He holds a Ph.D. in Human Resource Development from Barry University in Miami, FL. John is married with two children and two grandchildren.

John Curtis, Ph.D.
WWW.WECOHABITATE.COM
1.828.246.0459

MORE GREAT BOOKS TO ENHANCE YOUR LIFE!
Call in your order for fast service and quantity discounts!
(541) 347- 9882
OR order on-line at www.rdrpublishers.com using PayPal.
OR order by mail: Make a copy of this form; enclose payment information:
Robert D. Reed Publishers
1380 Face Rock Drive, Bandon, OR 97411

Name: _____

Address: _____

City: State: Zip: _____

Phone: Fax: Cell: _____

E-Mail: _____

Payment by check or credit card (All major credit cards are accepted)

Name on card: _____

Card Number: _____

Exp. Date: Last 3-Digit number on back of card: _____

Happily Un-Married: Living Together & Loving It!
by John Curtis, Ph.D. ….……..……………………….…… $16.95 _____
100 Ways to Create Wealth
by Steve Chandler and Sam Beckford …………………….. $24.95 _____
Why Am I So DAMN Unhappy?
by Jim Downton, Jr., Ph.D. ……………………………….…$11.95 _____
How Bad Do You Really Want It?
by Tom Massey ……………………………………….…….$19.95 _____
30 Days to a New You
by Monica Magnetti ……………………………………..….$19.95 _____
The Secret of Transitions
by Jim Manton …………………………………….……..….$14.95 _____
All You Need is HART!
by Helene Rothschild ……………………………….………$14.95 _____

Quantity: _____ Amount: _____
Shipping is $3.50 1st book + $1 for each add'l book: _____
Total Amount Enclosed: _____

Visit www.rdpublishing.com for more great titles!